FOOT-LOOSE
IN TOKYO

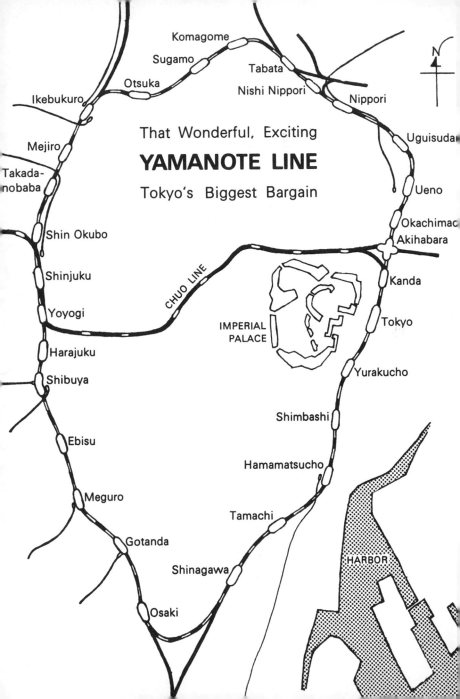

FOOT-LOOSE IN TOKYO

The Curious Traveler's Guide to the 29 Stages of the Yamanote Line

BY JEAN PEARCE

With Makiko Yamamoto and Fumio Ariga
Illustrations by Joy Harrison

NEW YORK   **WEATHERHILL**   TOKYO

First edition, 1976
Revised edition, fifth printing, 1993

Published by Weatherhill, Inc., of New York and Tokyo, with editorial offices at
420 Madison Avenue, 15th Floor, New York, N.Y. 10017. Protected by copyright
under the terms of the International Copyright Union; all rights reserved. Printed
in the U.S.A.

ISBN 0-8348-0123-X   LCC 76-23738

Contents

6 · Contents

Foreword

ONE OF THOSE EARLY DECISIONS which no one really understands very well and which have brought Japan great successes and great disasters this last hundred years had it that the Tokyo transportation system would be a mixture of public and private ownership. The decision had it further that transportation for the heart of the city would be in the public domain, and that privately owned lines could serve the suburbs but would not be admitted downtown. The result was a scattering of stations which then had to be joined if the suburban throngs were to get downtown at all. The result of the joining was the Yamanote Line, which serves in this book as an introduction to the city of Tokyo itself; indeed, it serves so admirably that one wonders at its having been neglected all these years.

Two and three decades ago the Yamanote had a single competitor, the Staten Island Ferry, as the finest nickel ride the world over. Today it is wholly without competitors as the finest dime ride. Soon it will be almost a quarter, but it will still be without competitors.*It is an interesting interpretation of the regulations that allows you to go so far for so little. Once you have bought your ticket for an adjacent station, say from Tokyo to Kanda, the next along the line, it doesn't matter whether you go directly there or make the almost full circle around the Yamanote loop. To get off halfway around is, strangely enough, a little more expensive, and if you do the full loop, you should alight at Kanda and buy another ticket for the short trip to the place where you started.

It is among the first things I did myself when I arrived in Tokyo.

* It is still a bargain even at today's increased fares.

I got an idea of the city by riding the Yamanote, and it therefore brings feelings of nostalgic satisfaction to find Jean Pearce and her associates suggesting the same device to others out to explore the city of Tokyo.

There were not then many high buildings near the tracks, and visibility from the Yamanote was better than it is today. There are cuts, however, where the line enters and departs from the hilly regions, and where visibility has always been zero. It was from one of them, near the top of the northern arc, that I first went up for a closer look. That first exploratory walk found me late one summer afternoon in 1948 gazing meditatively up at Sugamo Prison, wondering how many more sunrises and sunsets General Tojo had before him. The reader who turns to the chapter on Otsuka Station will find the answer to that question too in the remarkable wealth of information which is in this book. The fondness I have had ever since for Sugamo Prison stands as evidence of an important fact—that it is possible to become fond of almost anything in this extraordinary city.

Having first looked to see what might lie above those northwestern cuts, I set off at random to have a look at other places along the Yamanote, until I had a respectable knowledge of what the city contained. I did not close the circuit with anything like the systematic thoroughness of this book, and I wonder if my random method does not have much to recommend it. Ms. Pearce also favors a freedom to skip about in her book as whim or available time or personal interests may suggest. By jumping here and there along the Yamanote, one is made more aware of the variety the city contains than by moving systematically through neighborhoods only slightly different one from the next; and if there are disappointments, they are less likely to be repeated over on the far side of the circuit than at the next station up the line.

The variety is very great. Harajuku along the western sweep and Nippori at the northeast are at the extremes of today's Japan, the one with its boutiques and sports cars and flaming youth and the other with its temples and cemeteries and craftsmen devoted still to the ancient ways. Some of the stations—Uguisudani, for instance, the Yamanote stop serving the fewest customers—are as near quiet as anything in this teeming city, while Shinjuku is the busiest station in Japan, and doubtless one of the busiest in the world.

In the very origins of the Yamanote was assurance of variety. On its eastern course, chiefly the realm of the government railways, it pushes through the heart of the old city and along the line between the hills and flats that were the pre-modern abode of patrician and plebeian respectively. Along the west it joins the stations that serve the new suburbs. In the difference lies the fascination of the city, and the chief material for us its supporters in our running battle with supporters of Kyoto and Osaka. Kyoto may have pretty temples and gardens, we say, and Osaka has the puppet theater, but a person does not want that sort of thing day after day. Tokyo has everything. Despite a list of disasters such as few other cities can boast of and despite an affluent bourgeoisie madly in pursuit of Paris and New York, it has held on to a remarkable amount from the past.

My own preference, in all the variety, is for a run of a half dozen stations to the northeast, where lie the most extensive districts of the old city to escape fire bombings in World War II. It has been nice that few other foreigners have shared my preference. I almost never encounter one in the vicinity of, say, Nippori (while at Harajuku foreigners are legion). But it will be nice too if henceforth I come upon them in clusters, this book the badge of the little congregation we make. They will have come to Nippori for good reasons, and will have every right to be there. This book will have had the attention and the use it deserves.

Perhaps one day Ms. Pearce and her associates may be persuaded to extend the range of their endeavors. The chief thing wrong with the Yamanote is something that could not have been avoided—its shape. There the stations were and they had to be joined together;

the result was an ellipse, about twice as long on the north-south axis as on the east-west. The variety of the city is better displayed along the latter; and so, together with gratitude for the animating book we have before us, we may express the hope that the authors will one day apply their effective methods farther to the west, where boutiqueland is ever more so, and to the flatlands east of Ueno and on beyond the Sumida, where the child of old Tokyo goes on doing the old things.*

EDWARD SEIDENSTICKER

Spring, 1976

---

* And now they have, in *More Foot-loose in Tokyo!*

Author's Preface

THERE ARE MANY curious travelers in Japan. Some are visitors. Others live here. Yet there are more barriers than language to keep them from exploring the fascinating city around them. Not knowing what to see, where it is, how to get there, or what it is when one arrives—if indeed you do arrive—detracts much from the pleasure.

For many years I have wanted to write a guide to the Tokyo I have come to know and love, a book that would get people easily to where they wanted to go and tell them what they were seeing when they got there, a book that would lightly mix history and culture and entertainment with a good amount of practical information. But where to begin? How to give some logical organization to the disorganized jumble that Tokyo is? It was one day when riding on the Yamanote Line that encircles the heart of the city that I was suddenly reminded of how well Hiroshige had solved a similar problem many, many years ago with his magnificent series of woodblock prints called *The Fifty-three Stages on the Tokaido*. This book is the result. In a small way I have tried to do for Tokyo, in words, what Hiroshige did for the journey from Tokyo to Kyoto. Here we visit the areas surrounding the stations of the Yamanote Line—and incidentally meet the first of the many complications that make up Tokyo. You'll still hear old-time residents calling it the Yamate Line, but we'll use the name that's now been made official, with the pronunciation *yah-mah-no-tay*.

So take this book in hand and, by foot, rail—or armchair—start out—foot-loose and fancy-free, because I've made no hard and fast rules, set up no inflexible itineraries. Go wherever you want, see whatever you want to see, starting at whichever Yamanote station you like. To me, the first few stations are the most interesting. This is the center of old Tokyo, once known as Edo, and there's much remaining and reminding of those long ago, romantic days. If you can't find a place I talk about, try the accompanying map, or you can always ask for help by pointing to the Japanese writing in the text or in a footnote, and someone will send you off in the right direction. You may have to do this several times (and you may even find some friendly, helpful guide along the way), but in the end there you are! Success!

Some of the routes cover distances agreeable only to enthusiastic walkers. Then you may want to break the route into sections, or to supplement the rail system with an occasional taxi or bus. There are a number of places suggested for relaxing along the way.

Of course you don't *have* to take the tours at all. Just reading the book will help you understand the appeal of this sprawling, energizing city, and why so many people, although they speak longingly of their country origins, don't want to *live* any place else. It's always been that way, even when Tokyo was known as Edo.

Tokyo's vitality depends on variety. Beneath its smooth, unperturbed continuity, there are constant upheavals. Even before this book is off the presses, some information will be outdated, though only in small details. Old craftsmen will retire, restaurants will close (and open), and companies will relocate, but there'll always be something similar and perhaps even more interesting in their place—or just next door. Most of the places described, however, will still be there, along with the temples, shrines, and monuments, many with centuries of history already counted.

I should also add a few words about rush hours, when the normal definition of the word no longer applies and commuter trains are filled to twice or three times capacity. Do try to avoid the hours from about 8:00 to 9:30 in the morning and 5:00 to 6:30 in the evening. And yet, rush hours too are a part of the Yamanote story; try them once, or at least go and watch. Note, too, that most museums, galleries, and gardens are closed on Mondays.

As for the derivation of the station names, these are often obscure and open to question. So the literal translations I have given in English are more for local color than for scholarship. Don't try to use them when asking your way: you'll get only blank stares in reply.

And a final word of warning. This is a very personal guide. Thousands of pages could be written without finishing with Tokyo. I have mentioned only a few of the high spots that have interested me and that I believe will interest my readers. Other guidebooks are more methodical, often to the point of boredom. Here I hope I've kept moving fast enough to leave no time for yawning. And the person who joins me as I affectionately explore "my" city is sure to discover much that's new and different and fascinating, making it "his" or "her" city as well. How wonderful if we could all join hands in writing the book that will never be written—the definitive guide to Tokyo.

Years ago, in the early 1900s, someone wrote of the joys of traveling the Yamanote Line. He even recommended it for moon viewing (the Nikolai Cathedral drenched in moonlight, the wind blowing over the rice paddies that lined part of the route, far away from the crowded city). Obviously he knew a different Tokyo, but the point is still well made. A tour on the Yamanote Line is still a joyful introduction to the phenomenon called Tokyo.

A great many people have helped make this book possible. The list would certainly be headed by the Edokko, those long-ago "children of Edo" whose zest for living created the legends and history that are so well worth retelling today when their city has become Tokyo, one of the world's largest metropolises, with a new group of Edokko who, in turn, are busily weaving their own tales for tomorrow's history. And the modern list would surely begin with the Japanese National Railways: without their tirelessly efficient Yamanote Line this book could never have come into being.

I am also deeply grateful to my associates and collaborators. Mr. Fumio Ariga has been primarily responsible for the historical research. With his strong sense of history, his poet's heart, and his love for exploring his native city, he has provided the basic skeleton of the book, while also being largely responsible, together with the graphic designer Ms. Miho Miyazaki, for the maps.

Ms. Makiko Yamamoto, interpreter and translator, is known to many Westerners for her twenty-three years with the American Embassy in Tokyo and for her present position as a Lady-in-Waiting of the Imperial Household Agency. She has been the catalyst for the book, providing the essential union of languages and understanding.

Ms. Joy Harrison-Eguchi previewed the entire book in order to produce her charming ink drawings. Much as Hiroshige did along the Tokaido so long ago, she went back and forth along the Yamanote to find the precise spot from which to make each of her sketches.

And then there is my editor, Mr. Meredith Weatherby. Without his painstaking attention to words, clarity, and facts, the book could never have appeared in its present form. He joins me in apologizing for any oversights we both may have let slip by, and in hoping readers will supply corrections for future printings.

MITSUBISHI'S FIELD

Tokyo: Eastern Capital

TOKYO STATION IS an appropriate place to begin our tour of the city. Like Tokyo itself, this station has something for everyone.

Station shops profit by selling souvenirs from all over the country, an accommodation to travelers who do not like to be burdened with baggage. The service is also well patronized by the myriad Japanese businessmen who claim they're going to, say, Osaka for a business meeting when they are really spending the weekend—and usually not alone—at a hot-spring hideaway. Yet the evidence—an authentic Osaka souvenir—is there for all to see.

Beneath the east station and fanning out in all directions are

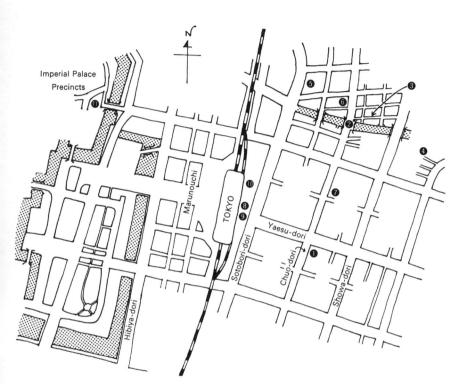

1. Bridgestone Museum
2. Nihon-bashi
3. William Adams Memorial
4. Tokyo Stock Exchange
5. Bank of Japan
6. Mitsukoshi Department Store
7. Takashimaya Department Store
8. Daimaru Department Store
9. Tetsudo Kaikan
10. Kokusai Kanko Kaikan
11. East Garden

hundreds of stores and restaurants and a great variety of services. You can buy the latest fashions, have a haircut, hear just-released recordings, check the latest stock-market quotations, or rent a cubicle with a flower name for a short rest. When this underground extravaganza first opened, street-level shops noticed an immediate decline in business. Owners formed a procession of protest with signs that said: "People are not moles! They should not live their lives below ground!"

But many people do spend minutes or hours a day underground in the shopping arcades and plazas and among the stairs and escalators that link the various commuter and long-distance trains, for Tokyo Station is one of the hubs of the nation's rail lines and the starting point for the high-speed Shinkansen to Kyoto and other points west. One and a half million people pass through the station each day.

Some six hundred of them stop daily for a bath at the Tokyo Onsen (東京温泉), one of the many deluxe bathhouses that dot the city, supplementing the many neighborhood public baths. The Tokyo Onsen, a branch of a well-known bathhouse of the same name in the Ginza area, is located within the station building. It's open from 5:30 a.m. to 10:30 p.m. The bath is a very important part of Japanese life (you will learn of other bathhouses in other chapters), and it is appropriate to have one here so people can refresh themselves after long journeys, or relax before starting home after a hard day in the city. The deluxe baths charge quite a bit more than the neighborhood baths. The latter used to supplement their modest charges by making women pay a few cents more on the theory that they used more soap and water in washing their long hair, but now that men's hair is almost as long they've had to bow to the times and charge the same for both sexes.

Leaving the station, you'll find the past in the nearby Imperial Palace and its parks. Occasional glimpses down narrow, willow-lined lanes will remind you of days when the streets were crowded, not with commuters, but with mile-long processions of kago (palanquins), retainers, samurai in full battle dress, and of course lovely ladies, for romance has always been a part of the local scene, whether our city is today's Tokyo, the Edo of shogun days, or a cluster of seaside villages.

The present is also very much in evidence, for this is the heart of the business and financial district with the head offices of many of Japan's largest enterprises and financial institutions. Some are built in areas whose names preserve the memory of the craftsmen who once had their shops here. Tokyo, always eager to engulf the latest fad or fancy, still maintains close links with its past.

Perhaps there should be a bit of background before starting our tour of Tokyo. Early history blends rustic strength with delicate sophistication, a frequent combination in Japan. Dokan Ota, a local chieftain, is worthy of note; not only did he found the city of Tokyo, in 1457, choosing a tiny fishing village called Edo on the Musashino plains as the vantage point for that new castle-fortress that would in time grow to be the present Imperial Palace, but he also exemplifies the way Japanese samurai could be at the same time both rough-and-ready warriors and men of great artistic sensibilities. The story goes, in Ota's case, that this came about in a very Japanese way. One day, riding through the countryside, he was caught in a sudden rainstorm. He asked a peasant girl (but mustn't she have been a lady-in-hiding, a princess from Kyoto exiled by some jealous wife, to judge from her actions?) to lend him a straw raincoat. For an answer, she handed him a spray of yellow roses, thereby expressing a subtle literary allusion. Ota, it is said, was so chagrined at his ignorance of classical poetry that he thereafter devoted himself to scholastic pursuits, combining the way of the warrior with the way of the aesthete and making Edo a center of refinement in the wilderness, thus setting a pattern that many were to follow. And—oh, yes, he never saw the girl again. In Japan few stories end with "and so they married and lived happily ever after."

With Ota's new castle, Edo grew to be an important military outpost during the next 150 years. Then, early in the 17th century, it was Ieyasu, the founder of the Tokugawa shogunate, that strange system of government under which the shoguns ruled while the emperors held court, who made what we now know as Tokyo the center of power in Japan. Defeating all rivals, Ieyasu wrested the seat of government away from overly refined Kyoto, home of the emperor, and dumped it down on Ota's Edo, an area previously viewed with disdain by the Kyoto nobility. (In 1464, upon reading one of Ota's poems, the emperor had remarked patronizingly that he did not know such sensitivity existed in Edo. The poem: "This house of mine / is in a grove of pines / beside a blue sea / and from under its rustic eaves / one sees high Fuji." There's probably no need to point out that most Japanese poems suffer in translation.)

When the Tokugawa rule was firmly established, the key was turned that locked Japan off from the rest of the world for two and a half centuries, resulting in the development of a distinctive and unique culture which lasted until the Meiji Restoration of 1868 restored power to the emperor. There are, however, those who maintain that no amount of contact with either West or East has significantly affected the Japanese way of life, and that even in to-day's Tokyo life goes on, under superficial differences, much as it did in Edo.

Turning back to our city, let's start with Yaesu, Tokyo Station's eastern exit. Explore, if you like, the mole-level shoppers' paradise. Almost any stairway or escalator will take you there, but proceed with care. There's no readable map to tell you where you might surface. But when you do . . .

Our first stop is the Bridgestone Museum[1] with its collection of 18th- and 19th-century Japanese and Western art. Bridgestone is well-known for tires and bicycles. The company was founded by Shojiro Ishibashi, who started by making rubber-soled shoes for workmen. His family name?—it means "bridge of stone."

Turn left for Nihon-bashi, Tokyo's most famous bridge, which also gives its name to the surrounding district. The first bridge was built here in 1603, the most recent one in 1911. Look at the northern end for a marker which commemorates the spot from which all distances in Japan were, and often still are, measured. A stone

---

1. Bridgestone Museum, 1–10–1 Kyobashi, Chuo-ku; tel. 563–0241
ブリジストン美術館　中央区京橋 1-10-1

memorial at the southern end pictures the original bridge. You will also find it among Hiroshige's print series of the fifty-three stages, or post towns, along the Tokaido, for this is where travelers began their journey along the legendary roadway that linked the shogun's Edo with the Emperor's Kyoto. Note the elaborate castiron lampposts that would still be a city landmark if the once-impressive bridge were not dwarfed by the overhead expressway.

(There is another monument you should look for, a tiny shrine near a red postbox, where the neighboring shopkeeper provides a daily offering: a glass of sake. It marks the location of the house of William Adams, the first Englishman to settle in Japan, in 1601. It was a decision forced upon him. His ship was wrecked, and he became an adviser to Ieyasu, teaching him such exotic arts as gunnery, geography, and mathematics. You may know him better as John Blackthorne in Richard Clavell's *Shogun*, or as the needle watcher in Richard Blaker's biography.)

To the right is the Tokyo Stock Exchange (東京証券取引所), popularly known as Kabuto-cho from the name of the section in which it is located. To the left are the main offices of the Bank of Japan (日本銀行), the country's central bank, dominant in political and financial circles. It had an early start: in Ieyasu's day, gold coins were minted here. Visitors will be given a tour of the exchange, and you only need to walk in to have a look at the prestigious Bank of Japan. Numismatists should ask to see the bank's extensive collection of coins. You'll find it in the old building, a formidable piece of granite architecture that has been designated an Important Cultural Asset, right next to the imposing new building.

The best introduction to modern Japanese life is a visit to a department store, and two of the finest, Mitsukoshi and Takashimaya, are located in the Nihon-bashi district, one on each side of the bridge. Mitsukoshi is Japan's oldest. It got its start early in the 17th century, first as a draper's shop called Echigoya established by the Mitsui family of provincial bankers, when daimyo—feudal lords—

from the provinces, in need of money to meet expenses in the capital, began entrusting their funds to Echigoya. With a flair for business unique in those times, Echigoya would buy merchandise with the funds and bring it to the city, where it was sold at greatly inflated prices. Thus the daimyo would receive back their money, and Echigoya would count its profits. The family still counts profits today, but under a different name: it has grown to become the world-renowned Mitsui conglomerate, and Mitsukoshi is the descendant of that small draper's shop.

Choose either Mitsukoshi or Takashimaya for a floor-by-floor tour. Start with the basement food department, wondering if they really eat *that*, whatever it is, and progress to the top floor exhibition halls. There you may see the most extensive collection of some famous Western artist's work that has ever been brought together in one place—or discover hundreds of Japanese from teenagers in jeans and T-shirts to their elders in impeccable kimono viewing with silent awe a rare exhibition of fabulously expensive garden stones, of far more worth to many Japanese than the finest works of Western art.

For another experience you will always remember, be at the store when the doors open, usually 10 a.m. You will be greeted by the staff as the most honored guest, and the ceremony will be repeated at each floor as you ride up on the escalator.

Back at the station, another good introduction to Japan can be had by visiting the display rooms of local products that most of the prefectures have set up; some of these are above the Daimaru Department Store, on the ninth floor of the Tetsudo Kaikan,[2] and others in the Kokusai Kanko Kaikan[3] next door, floors one through four. You will see crafts and products from all over the country.

2. Tetsudo Kaikan, 1–9–1 Marunouchi, Chiyoda-ku; tel. 231–0953
   鉄道会館　千代田区丸ノ内 1-9-1
3. Kokusai Kanko Kaikan, 1–8–3 Marunouchi, Chiyoda-ku; tel. 215–1181
   国際観光会館　千代田区丸ノ内 1-8-3

Spend a few thousand yen and you'll have a fascinating collection, all attractively packaged for easy carrying or mailing.

A passageway under the tracks will take you to the Marunouchi side of the station. Once the area between the Imperial Palace and what is now the station was a military parade ground, but after the Meiji Restoration it was selected to be the business center. It was decided to sell the land to raise the necessary money for the project. The purchaser was Yanosuke Iwasaki, then the head of Mitsubishi Company. (You'll meet his brother at a garden near Komagome Station.) He paid one and a half million yen for the property. Some criticized his lack of business acumen in spending so vast a fortune for such weed-covered, undeveloped land. Mitsubishi's field, they called it, but Iwasaki reportedly just smiled and said, "Well, if nothing else, we can plant bamboo and raise tigers," a remark that has been handed down by his admirers, who today see the tigers of Marunouchi extending their power and products throughout the world. During the war, Mitsubishi's roofs—those that survived the bombings—were used for growing potatoes. Now, new headquarters buildings for Mitsubishi enterprises line the streets, the best-kept in the city. They are still owned by Mitsubishi, who laid the area out long ago for Japan's future business center using London's Lombard Street as a model. Alas, the lovely red-brick buildings with their mansard roofs have now given way to steel and cement and glass, but a look at the station building itself will give a faint idea how the entire area used to look.*

Many wonder at the unusual architectural style of the old Tokyo Station (to be seen from the Marunouchi side), though it would not seem strange to residents of Amsterdam, for that was the station building the builders used for their inspiration. Construction got under way in 1908, but the building wasn't completed until 1914. There was an up-to-the-minute hotel on the second and third floors.

---

* If it is still there.

People came from all over the country to admire the extravagant facilities that had been built at a tremendous cost.

The building was extensively damaged in World War II. It was promptly repaired, but in the process it lost its third floor and its two much-admired domed roofs. What the future holds in store for the old building has not yet been determined. Sentimentalists want to keep it, others want to replace it with a new skyscraper. In fact, the plans were drawn up more than ten years ago, but there wasn't enough money to carry them out. The effort was not wasted, however. Tokyo's first skyscraper, the Kasumigaseki Building (at Toranomon, near the U.S. Embassy), was based on the research carried out for the new Tokyo Station Building.

The hotel is still there, and the second floor restaurant-in-the-round still provides top-quality food in old surroundings that will remind you of other days as you watch the trains come and go . . . come and go . . . and come and go. . . . If you counted long enough, you'd find that some 2,680 trains use Tokyo Station every day.

Beyond the station is the Imperial Palace. Once, when the shoguns called it home, it extended over much of the city, and the huge stones that comprise the walls had to be brought, two to a boat, all the way from the Izu Peninsula. It's said that it took one hundred men to move each stone. In time, it's claimed, it became the largest castle in the world when judged by the land it covered. The enrichment of the palace was done with a purpose. Expenses were borne by the daimyo, the feudal lords who ruled the provinces and were periodically required to make large contributions on the sound theory that a financially pressed lord could not gather the necessary legions to launch a revolt.

Visitors can enter the palace grounds on January 2 and on the emperor's birthday. Then great crowds cross the Niju-bashi bridge to greet their symbolic head of state with rising-sun flags and shouts of "Banzai!" It is possible, sometimes, to make arrangements to visit the palace grounds by requesting permission well in advance from the Imperial Household Agency.

Always open, except on Mondays and Fridays, is the East Garden, once a part of the original castle grounds. But that was a long time ago. You'll learn a lot more about those days as our train takes us, station by station, on the curious traveler's guide to both Edo and Tokyo.

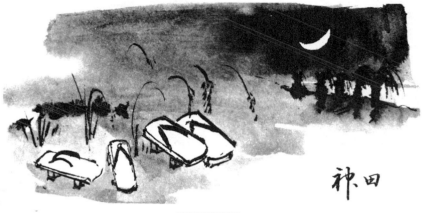

神田

RENDEZVOUS

Kanda: God's Rice Field

As you wonder which of the many angling streets to follow when you leave Kanda Station, you may not find it believable, but Kanda was in fact one of the first planned communities of Edo days. Obviously, planning had a different connotation then. The idea, often followed since, was to bring together people of the same profession. In the case of Kanda, they were all craftsmen, and even today they are remembered in district names such as Kaji-cho, where the blacksmiths worked, and Konya-cho, for dyers. There is still a Norimono (riding-on-thing) -cho, though the demand for its products has long

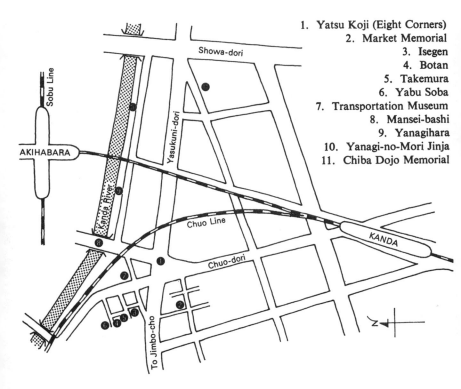

1. Yatsu Koji (Eight Corners)
2. Market Memorial
3. Isegen
4. Botan
5. Takemura
6. Yabu Soba
7. Transportation Museum
8. Mansei-bashi
9. Yanagihara
10. Yanagi-no-Mori Jinja
11. Chiba Dojo Memorial

since ceased; the men who lived there were makers of kago, the Japanese form of palanquin.

To the west of the station were the walls of Edo Castle. Naturally, this area just outside the castle was a center of trade and barter, for catering to the castle's needs was the major occupation in those early days. Today's caterers are clustered around the station, serving soba (noodles) and domburi (rice topped with a variety of mixtures) to commuters and the quick-lunch crowd from the many small wholesale shops located along the winding streets. Trade and catering remain a principal activity of Kanda.

Walk along Chuo-dori, the main street in front of the station. If it's nice weather, sidewalk stands will be heaped high with the day's bargains. You'll pass many yard-goods shops, all featuring the best prices in town. On the right side, a store crowded with customers sells Japanese-style pickled vegetables, on the left you'll pass a tiny shop where a man sits on a raised tatami-matted platform just inside an attractive stone-and-wood-lined entranceway, serenely threading toe straps into geta soles. Yes, like shoes, geta and zori should be properly fitted, even though the only fit is in the tightness of the strap between the toes.

Soon you'll reach Yatsu Koji (Eight Corners). Don't try to count them. There will be more or less depending on how far you extend the corner.

Once a famous bathhouse/teahouse stood here. The Japanese way of coining words is well demonstrated by its name, Tanzen-buro: *tan* came from the name of the lord, Tango no Kami, whose mansion stood across the street, while *zen* means "in front of" and *buro*, "bath"—in short, the bath in front of Tango's. The men who came here swaggered about in padded kimono furnished by the bathhouse to be worn while resting after the bath. These too became known as tanzen, as they still are today; the name became a part of the nation's vocabulary. At the bathhouse, with its friendly waitresses, bath and bed were closely associated. But after a pleasant interval, it was back to work again, for while these men were known for their bathhouse romances, they worked as hard as they played.

It was the apprentice system of the day that ruled their lives. Seldom could a man consider marriage until he was well past thirty. His first loyalty was to his master and he was constantly at the master's service except for those few moments of bravado at the bath. There was no time for a young man to have a wife and family of his own.

But we'll leave this, a memory well camouflaged by today's traffic and congestion. Turn left just before Eight Corners. You are at the beginning of the vegetable market of old Edo. Here produce from all over the country was brought in by boat and displayed on the embankment alongside the Hira River (really a canal). Streets were filled with gaily decorated carts piled high with bright-colored vegetables being pulled by young men dressed in white and carrying banners proclaiming just whose goods were being taken to the palace for the shogun's pleasure. This, they say, was the beginning of the Kanda Festival, one of Edo's (and Tokyo's) most famous yearly events, about which we'll have more to say in the Akihabara chapter.

Along the street on the right you'll find a stone marker that records the history of the market and its final end, when it was leveled in the great earthquake of 1923. Do notice the old house-office behind the marker. The elderly gentleman who owns it is still active in the vegetable wholesale business.

Take the next right. You may notice a small sweetshop on the left. It has a number of loyal customers. A popular sumo umpire opened it after he retired. At the back of the store are a few mementos of his sumo days.

This area is noted for its traditional restaurants. Isegen (いせ源), famous for fish cookery, and Botan (ぼたん), known for its chicken specialties, and Bandai-ya (万代や), set in the corner of a picture perfect old ryokan (foreigners accomodated), all serving lunch and dinner. Takemura[1] is a sweetshop renowned for its deep-fried manju, served hot from the fire. This bun-and-bean paste delicacy was a favorite of Edo days, but few Tokyo shops continue the tradition. Please note that when you have a Japanese-type sweet it is always accompanied by a free cup of green tea; have a Western sweet and your bill is more than doubled by your cup of coffee.

Yabu Soba[2] serves its excellent noodles in a beautiful old country-style building surrounded by graceful bamboos. Kimono-clad

1. Takemura, 1–19 Kanda Suda-cho, Chiyoda-ku; tel. 251–2328
   竹村　千代田区神田須田町 1–19
2. Yabu Soba, 2–10 Kanda Awaji-cho, Chiyoda-ku; tel. 251–0287
   やぶそば　千代田区神田淡路町 2–10

waitresses will call out your order to the cooks in the open kitchen, all in Edo style. A specialty is a seafood fritter called kaki-age, often eaten with cold soba. This is a nice place to share with visitors from abroad who want to experience a bit of the elusive old Japan. After lunch, take them to Takemura's for a dessert of fried manju—ask for age-manju. Show how knowledgeable you are by pointing out that the shops are owned by brothers.

Now on to the Transportation Museum (Kotsu Hakubutsukan, 交通博物館). At first you might think it's only buses that are on display, but they are there as visitors, having brought in endless groups of touring students.

Several of the museum's exhibits are outdoors. The brightly decorated yellow train car was once pulled by an engine named Benkei (made in Pittsburgh), on display nearby. It was operated in Hokkaido back in 1880. This was the latest in luxury. You could wind the windows up and down and the seats could be reversed. The old bus you'll see was the first ever made in Japan—the year, 1930. When you remember that the first train in Japan began service in 1872 (and you can see "Engine Number 1," which pulled it between Tokyo and Yokohama), you will realize how fast Japan has progressed in the field of transportation—Japanese automobiles familiar throughout the world, the highspeed Shinkansen. You'll find this short history recorded at the museum, appropriately housed within a building made up in part of the red brick arches that once served to support the elevated railway tracks.

Now cross the Hira River by way of the bridge known as Mansei-bashi. An earlier bridge at that spot was built of the great stones from a gate tower of Edo Castle. The land from Mansei-bashi running along the river was once the poor man's Yoshiwara, the famous Asakusa pleasure quarter. The section is still known as Yanagihara (Willow Fields). Here, along the river, there was bargaining for the goods brought in by the Kanda waterway. At night, there was bargaining of another kind, for this was the haunt of the yotaka (night hawks), the name given to the prostitutes who made these streets their hunting grounds. Beyond the willows were the rice fields where they led their willing customers. The price was right for poor farmers, tradesmen, and apprentices—only twenty-four of the small copper coins called mon, whereas girls at the shukuba (the inns of the post towns) wouldn't accept less than two hundred mon. New Year's Eve was a busy time for the yotaka. One girl, after a most successful year-end, changed her name to Hitotose (One Year), for she claimed she had had 365 customers that night. Men who sold soba from carts were also called yotaka because they came out at night and their prices were cheap.

Later this area became the center for used-kimono sales, and during the early days of the Occupation, when, for the Japanese, food was much more important than adornment, many foreigners picked up family treasures here for a small fraction of their actual worth. Now it's a wholesale area for yard goods, ready-to-wear, and supplies for tailors and dressmakers.

One last stop as you return to the station, Yanagi-no-Mori Jinja (柳森神社, Willow Grove Shrine), one you could pass easily without noticing, for it is located well below street level. Once this was the site of a huge rice-storage center; it was used to supply the needy in one of the city's first welfare programs. The shrine is noted for its weightlifters, who used stones instead of barbells. The largest stone was lifted by an early sumo wrestler (and it's said that one of his descendants won an Olympic weightlifting award). Each stone is marked with the name of the man who lifted it, along with the names of witnesses.

On the way back to the station, you'll pass the former site of the Chiba Dojo, a famous kendo school. A memorial tablet has been erected within the entranceway of the primary school that is now located there. Kendo is not one of its subjects.

You are not far from Demma-cho, its name a reminder of Demma Prison that once stood there. It's told how prisoners were released whenever the area was threatened by the frequent fires that so often leveled Edo. They had to promise to return after the fire was put out. In spite of the confusion and the huge numbers of unidentified dead, they did. The tragic story of one of these conflagrations is told in the Sugamo chapter.

WASHING MACHINES WASHING

Akihabara: Field of Autumn Leaves

THERE'S HARDLY ANYONE who doesn't know what Akihabara is famous for. Maybe long, long ago it was a field of autumn leaves, but today it is Tokyo's wholesale district for electric/electronic products, which are also sold retail at cut-rate prices. Lined up along the main streets are all kinds of audio equipment, appliances, and lighting fixtures; search the back streets and alleys for parts. Bargaining is in order in the smaller shops, and pocket calculators will figure a balance between your offer and the store's profit as abacuses once did. If it's electrical and available in Japan, you're likely to find it here. It is a scene of agitated motion and sound: washing machines washing, TVs televising, and fans blowing or heaters heating depending on the season. Some shops have electronic voices that welcome you, "Irasshai, come in, bargains. . . ." One of the largest, Yamagiwa,[1] is a department store of appliances. Many stores feature merchandise made for export. Shop carefully to be sure that volts and cycles are correct for your country. One of the best: LAOX's duty-free corner.[2]

The bargains that attract customers today are often electronic marvels, family computers for mother and dad, and space-age toys for the children. (Clap your hands and watch the toy that young Jiro made change direction as its sound sensor responds to the noise.) Japan's children will be well prepared for the future. There is very little that can challenge them beyond the computerized toys they play with today.

But our immediate destination, far removed in time from Akihabara's bargains, is Kanda Myojin (神田明神), a Shinto shrine dating back, it is claimed, to the mid-8th century. The present main shrine, vermilion colored, was completed in 1934 after its most recent catastrophe, the 1923 earthquake, though it had experienced many earlier destructions. At the entranceway is a shop famous for pickles and miso (fermented bean paste), the main ingredient of the soup that's as important for a Japanese breakfast as is the morning cup of coffee in America. And the pickles! Even if you think you don't like these Japanese delicacies, buy a bag or two to sample. Try the baby eggplants in mustard or the sweet-hot ginger.

Behind the main building are mini-shrines, some holding the omikoshi that are carried through the streets during the shrine's famous Kanda Festival held in May, others dedicated to various

1. Yamagiwa Denki, 4–1–1 Soto Kanda, Chiyoda-ku; tel. 253–2111
   ヤマギワ電気　千代田区外神田 4–1–1
2. LAOX, 1–2–9 Soto Kanda, Chiyoda-ku; tel. 255–9041
   ラオックス　千代田区外神田 1-2-9

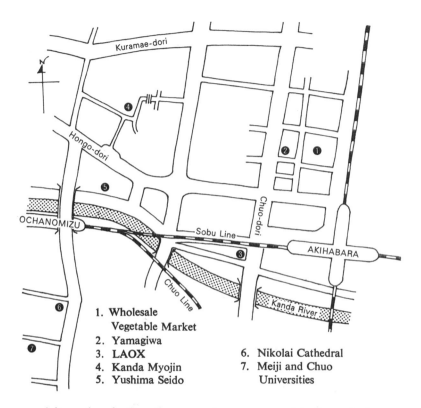

1. Wholesale Vegetable Market
2. Yamagiwa
3. LAOX
4. Kanda Myojin
5. Yushima Seido
6. Nikolai Cathedral
7. Meiji and Chuo Universities

spirits and gods. One, for example, pays respect to the god of woven baskets. There is also a stone monument to Heiji Zenigata, a famous Edo detective, presented by the actors who play his part in today's popular TV dramas.

From the top of the steep steps at the side of the shrine, you can't see much. In the old days, this was a famous height. Why, you could see all the way to Chiba from here, and fishing boats heading for Edo set their course by the green of the ginkgo trees that covered this hilltop. Three old ginkgoes remain. They are now under government protection.

Below, the angling roofs of a few old-style geisha houses with pretty gates and gardens are a reminder of other days, when tradesmen who sold their produce in the Kanda markets were entertained in a fashion far more sophisticated than what they knew back home in the provinces.

Next comes Yushima Seido (湯島聖堂), a shrine dedicated to the Chinese sage Confucius, whose teachings have had great influence in Japan. At the entrance is a large library building for the study of Confucian ethics. This building also used to house an antique shop much favored by bargain hunters in postwar years, but the shop has moved elsewhere, leaving the scholars to their peace and quiet.

Behind the library is the somber but impressive shrine itself. The first shrine building was erected here in 1690 by Tsunayoshi, the fifth Tokugawa shogun, though the present building dates back only to 1935, the former ones having been repeatedly leveled by fires. Many famous scholars and statesmen of the shogunate received their Confucian education here. The early school of ethics is recognized as one of the forerunners of Tokyo University.

From the hill you can see the dome of Nikolai Cathedral, the Japanese Orthodox church, completed in 1884. This was an architectural form new to Japan in those days, and a number of people were said to have objected strenuously to the construction. They felt the high dome could have only one purpose: to spy, from that high vantage point, on the emperor's palace and the activities of the city. It too was rebuilt after the 1923 earthquake.

A little miracle was enacted here a few years ago. The bishop, thinking of the high costs and his limited budget, was considering which of the church's most urgent repairs should be undertaken. He turned to find a stranger at the door. "I have some money for the church," the man said, thrusting an envelope into the bishop's hands as he left, never to be seen again. It was a very large amount, and an instant decision was made—to install stained-glass windows in the sanctuary, a long-cherished wish. But who could do it?

That afternoon the bishop stopped at a coffee shop and noticed a striking stained-glass window above the counter. He asked the name of the person who had created it. As soon as he returned to his office, he called the craftsman and explained his project. There was a strange sound—was it a sob?—at the other end of the line. It seems that the artist had also had a dream. He had been a boy of fourteen, an apprentice glassmaker, at the time of the earthquake. He had greatly admired the old cathedral and had been saddened by its destruction. Later he made a model of the new building, adding the brilliant stained-glass windows he thought it should have. Through the years he had kept the model on his desk, a constant inspiration for his work. Surely there is no need to tell you that the project was successfully completed, and the windows show the extra beauty that is always apparent in the work of those dealing in miracles. Christmas and Easter provide an opportunity for visitors to admire this miracle.

Jimbo-cho is not far away. The area has always been a popular place for browsing, for it is Tokyo's center for new and used books. Dealers congregated here because many universities were located nearby. Now the schools are gradually moving into less-crowded areas, but the book dealers remain. Old, dusty buildings have been modernized, and cultural activities such as art shows and film festivals are sponsored, in an effort to attract new customers. There are still bargains to be found in old books, and many people, both Japanese and foreign, seek them out on the well-filled shelves of Jimbo-cho.

If you have wandered this far from the Yamanote Line, you might try a rival system of transportation for your return. How about the subway? Jimbo-cho is a station on the Toei Mita (No. 6 Municipal) Line with stops at Otemachi, Hibiya, and Mita, as well as on the Shinjuku Line that cuts across town to the western side of the Yamanote Line; you can also take the Marunouchi Line at Ochanomizu Station, which you passed on your way to Nikolai Cathedral.

御徒町

SEEKING FAVORS

Okachimachi: Honorable Walkers Town

OKACHIMACHI HAS ALWAYS BEEN a proletarian district but one which nevertheless marks its name with an honorific *o*. This is the section of Edo where the kachigumi, the lowest rank of samurai, once lived. *Gumi* means "group," and the *kachi* were the samurai who walked—the ones not authorized to ride horses—in the tightly categorized society of early Japan. All daimyo had samurai-who-walked, but only those serving under the shogun received the honorific *o* before their name. These infantrymen of the shogun are remembered today in the station's name.

There must have been a great number of them. The streets of

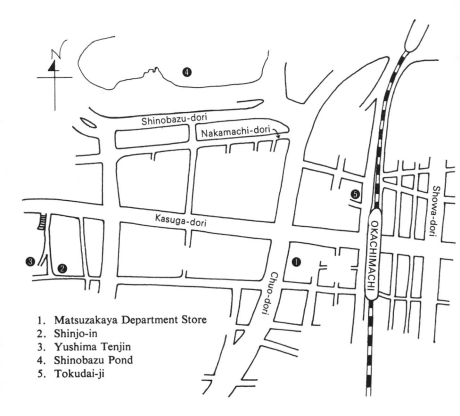

1. Matsuzakaya Department Store
2. Shinjo-in
3. Yushima Tenjin
4. Shinobazu Pond
5. Tokudai-ji

nearby Akihabara, now filled with people searching for bargains in electrical goods, were once the destination of these poor but proud men seeking genteel entertainment appropriate to their station. It's said that the morning-glory market (described in the Uguisudani chapter) had its beginnings in the popular hobby of the kachigumi, who trained morning-glory plants to grow in fanciful shapes, much as the nobility trained bonsai (dwarf trees).

One would suppose that the kachigumi suffered from the lack of horses during the feudal period. They suffered a great deal more after the Meiji Restoration, for their talents had little value in a world without samurai. Their profession was guard duty for the shogun and now there were no openings in their field.

Some tried trade in the area they knew best and set up shops in Okachimachi. Few of them succeeded; their past experience had little to contribute to their new occupation. The location, however, proved right for marketing, and as they failed, their shops were taken over by more experienced merchants and Okachimachi's reputation was soon firmly established—a cut-price market area where you could always find a bargain.

It hasn't changed much. There are plenty of bargains for those who come to Okachimachi to fill shopping bags with a variety of goods that would defy cataloguing. But watch the price tags. Not everything is a bargain and the shopper who can make price comparisons does best. If you have a penchant for bargaining, this is a good place to practice your skill. Your talents may not always be rewarded, but it is an acceptable place to try.

"What will I find there?" you ask. Well, start in the covered area under the tracks. Clustered around the entrance you'll see a number of shops with bargains in golf clubs, clothes, and accessories. Many Japanese select what they want at department stores, then come to Okachimachi to search out the same, but at lower prices.

You'll benefit from a crash course in kanji for shopping. Otherwise you may hand the salesman ¥2,000 for a golf shirt that might seem like a bargain to you. And the salesman might accept your money, not bothering to point out that the sign on the display case says fifty percent off the marked price.

There's one sign you'll recognize. It says "McDonald Hamburgers," a nod to modern marketing in this old-fashioned shopping area.

We won't attempt to provide a guide for your exploration, but will point out a few truths. When you find something you want, buy it. It may not be there tomorrow; or it may be there but you won't be able to find the shop. If you must postpone your decision, be sure to get a meishi (name card) and write on it in English so that later, when you need it, you'll know whose card it is. Then when you do come back, you'll be able to show it and be pointed toward your destination by other shopkeepers, helpful even though they may be competitors, a courtesy not common to all countries.

Somewhere in the maze of Okachimachi you'll find just about everything that is sold in the shops of Japan. Its two feature attractions, however, are timepieces and jewelry. There are more than seventy shops that sell everything from cheap novelty wrist watches —Mickey Mouse? Alice in Wonderland?—to imported Audemars-Piquets with majestic price tags. As for the jewelry, costume types are most obvious, but more discriminating shoppers can find bargains in high-value jewels. Unlike this kind of market in other countries, Okachimachi is a place where you can be reasonably sure of quality as advertised, and if you do have complaints, the shop will likely be there when you return. Save that meishi.

Another specialty is "military surplus," the quotation marks because most of it is manufactured to meet today's civilian demand; a more accurate term would be manufacturer's surplus. There are bargains to be had in luggage, handbags, and clothing. You'll also find imported goods, including some that you won't see elsewhere. Several shops carry a wide variety of what appear to be expensive guns. None of these, however, will ever fire a bullet even though the "ammunition" is also on sale. Japan has strict gun-control laws; gun fanciers must settle for realistic copies.

Visit the shops lining the street for bargains in food, all the essentials for the Japanese table as well as a wide selection of Western products. You'll hear the "Irasshai!" (welcome) call of the fish salesmen, you'll discover rare imported fruit (some just short of being overripe). It doesn't take a pocket calculator to show that prices are much cheaper than those you are accustomed to paying. Some budget-conscious shoppers make trips here once or twice a month to fill shelves and freezers.

Now imagine another day, right after World War II. Okachimachi's stalls were filled with other goods: black-market rice and fruit and vegetables. People bartered family treasures for food that would perhaps be only enough for one hearty meal, though it would likely be stretched over a day or a week. Later, a new look, but still a black market. It was at Okachimachi that many Japanese first learned about foreign products as they selected from a stunning array of consumer goods somehow siphoned off from PX supplies, exotic luxuries for the Japanese after wartime paucity. The area alongside the tracks between Okachimachi and Ueno is still known as Ameyoko; some say it means "Town of American Sidestreets."

Okachimachi was not all market stalls. The first Matsuzakaya was established here in 1707 to make the robes for the priests at Kan'ei-ji temple. Some sixty years later it was expanded into a gofukuten (dry-goods store) and later still into a hyakkaten (one-hundred-goods store), the word used for department stores before *depato* became a part of everyone's vocabulary.

Follow the street that passes between the two buildings of Matsuzakaya Hyakkaten to the overhead and cross the wide street. Even in Edo days this was an impressive thoroughfare—it was created as a firebreak after one of the city's disastrous conflagrations. It has always been known as Hirokoji (Big Road).

Look down the cross-streets for occasional glimpses of old Japan, scenes to remind you of other days: small, well-kept doorway gardens, occasional old signs, brown wood antiqued by time, and on almost every house an incongruous bright red mailbox.

The street ends in a flight of steps leading up to a shrine called Yushima Tenjin (湯島天神), which traces its history back some six centuries. When Edo was a fishing village, the farmers of nearby Yushima erected a shrine here to honor the god of learning. The approach is guarded by a small temple, Shinjo-in, with a willow-edged pool inhabited by a large number of turtles. As you climb the steep steps, you may reflect on the fact that shrines seek out high places with large trees. The hill is known as Otoko-zaka (Male Slope). Naturally you will find an Onna-zaka (Female Slope) nearby. You may be interested in a discussion of several years ago as to whether Mount Fuji should be referred to as *he* or *she*. A compromise was reached: its strong, steep slope is male, the gentler one, female. Japan, its roots deep in the nature-wonder of Shinto, knows you can't have one without the other.

Once, sad but hopeful people came to Yushima Tenjin to post their messages on a maigo-ishi (lost-child stone). There were three such stones in Edo where people could leave notices describing children lost from their parents, a common occurrence in days when fires frequently burned out large sections of the city. The Yushima stone still stands, encircled by a low fence, but no one leaves messages there anymore. Instead, students (or their parents) come from all over Japan to pray to the god of learning for admission to the school of their choice. Some start early, hoping for entrance to prestigious kindergartens.

The strange building on stilts that you'll see is really a roof that protects, but not very well, a collection of paintings on wood: votive tablets known as ema. Near the shrine building is a huge collection of small ema left there by worshipers seeking favors.

Do pause before going back down the steps to admire the variety of roofs stretching out below, a pleasing vista of colors and angles, and the distant view of Shinobazu Pond at Ueno Park. If it is early spring, you won't have to be told that Yushima is famous for its plum blossoms. If it's another season, remember to come back next spring.

We are told that Utamaro, the renowned woodblock-print artist, once lived near Okachimachi Station. He must have stood on this very hill, perhaps composing mental images of the Edo that we see today in his prints.

Return to the station and find, on the Ueno side, another temple, though you may not recognize it as one. This is Tokudai-ji (徳大寺), rebuilt to meet the needs of changing times. There are restaurants in the basement and on the first floor; the temple is on the second. It is dedicated to the female deity Marishiten, the guardian of samurai setting out for battle. Today you may find a man about to place his bet on the horses (or a gangster? a member of the revolutionary Sekigun?) requesting her blessing. Or perhaps it's just a concerned commuter, off to do battle with Tokyo's transportation network during the rush hour.

TRUANT DRAGONS

Ueno: Upper Plain

ANY TOKYO GUIDEBOOK, including this one, will contain a map
showing Ueno Park, a cultural conglomerate providing an awesome
variety of diversions. But ours is no definitive guide for you to go
to sleep over, and here too we'll only point out a few things you
might otherwise overlook. Or perhaps it would be more accurate
to say, things we ourselves have especially liked or wondered about.

Directly across from the nearest Yamanote exit is the Tokyo Metropolitan Festival Hall, whose acoustics have been praised by famous
maestros, among them the Philadelphia Orchestra's demanding
Eugene Ormandy. Beyond are museums and art galleries (Eastern

and Western, contemporary and ancient, and points between), a university of the arts, temples, shrines, memorials, a zoo, and a great deal more. Come often to Ueno. You'll have to, to follow all the paths, to visit all the exhibits.

Once Ueno Park was only a bluff overlooking the sea. (Almost anywhere you go in downtown Tokyo, keep in mind that many areas that look as though they'd always been there have actually been reclaimed from Tokyo Bay in modern times.) We're told that when Edo was still young, bamboo was brought all the way from China to beautify the Ueno hills. Daimyo built their residences here, and later these gave way to temples until the hillside must have resembled an ethereal scroll painting with curved roofs and lacquered buildings glimpsed among pine and bamboo. It became a favored place of worship and relaxation for the Tokugawa shoguns.

Though little remains, all has not been lost. There is Kiyomizudo (清水堂), whose faded and peeling red-lacquer coat testifies to its age, a copy, it's claimed, of the magnificent Kiyomizu Temple in Kyoto. It was hoped to create the same feeling of massive splendor here, but nothing came of that. The Kyoto original, built impressively on piles, fills a space between mountains. The toy copy at Ueno is perched on a low hill called a mountain only by the poetic, the wooden supports merely unnecessary decorations.

It does, however, have its own tradition. Women who have had babies come to Kiyomizu with their infants and leave token dolls behind as protectors of the children's health. You will see them piled around a small altar on the left, a somewhat surprising collection because most are what Japanese consider Western dolls. One would rather expect to find traditional Japanese images at a Buddhist altar. Once a year, on September 25, the collection is ceremoniously burned, and a new one started.

From the balcony there is a pleasing view of Shinobazu Pond, which once was part of a clear lagoon stretching to the sea. During the war, it was turned into a rice paddy. Now it is almost choked

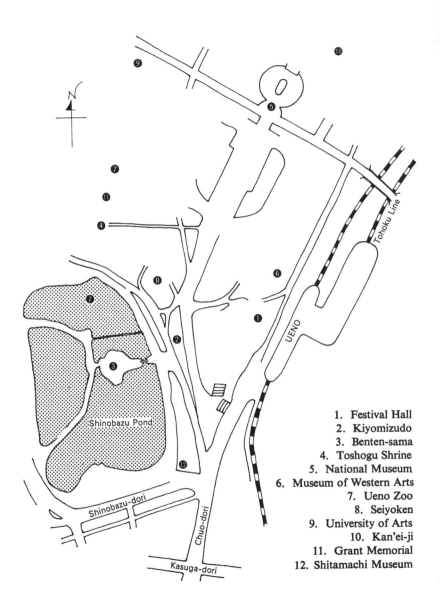

1. Festival Hall
2. Kiyomizudo
3. Benten-sama
4. Toshogu Shrine
5. National Museum
6. Museum of Western Arts
7. Ueno Zoo
8. Seiyoken
9. University of Arts
10. Kan'ei-ji
11. Grant Memorial
12. Shitamachi Museum

Shinobazu Pond

Shinobazu-dori

Chuo-dori

Kasuga-dori

UENO

Tohoku Line

N

with lotus plants and pollution. Frogs are frequently released here by sentimental people who hope to recreate the sounds of the country so valued in the city. Few reach adulthood. In July and August a plant fair is held around the pond and a fantastic array of trees, rocks, bonsai, flowers, shrubs, and plants are brought by gardeners to sell to yukata-dressed visitors who recreate an evening in Edo as they stroll along the lantern-lit paths.

In the center of the pond is the island temple of Benten-sama (弁天堂), guardian divinity of the arts, a jealous goddess whom lovers should avoid, for she has the power to change a happy romance into a disaster. To the left is a stone tablet with a carved figure of a blowfish (fugu). It is in memory of all the fish that have been savored by connoisseurs who relish this form of culinary Russian roulette. There should be another monument to those humans who have lost their lives in pursuit of this risky pleasure. Improperly cleaned fugu causes almost-certain quick death, and a number of fugu parties end in a funeral. The government imposes strict examinations for all restaurant attendants who prepare blowfish. If you have fugu at an approved shop, you are always sure that what you are served is safe. Well, almost always. . . .

At the pond's edge is the Shitamachi Museum (下町風俗資料館) full of memories and mementos from Tokyo's past. The first floor features street scenes that only need people for reality, the second displays a pleasing variety of everyday things, many contributed by the present residents of what is left of Shitamachi.

The builders of Edo must have felt little confidence in their own architectural designs for there is another copy: Toshogu Shrine (東照宮), a tiny bit of Nikko at the end of a path lined with stone lanterns.

Toshogu too has a legend. There was concern in the old days about the two carved dragons on the gate. Every morning they were

1. Shitamachi Museum, 2–1 Ueno Koen, Taito-ku; tel. 823–7451
   下町風俗資料館　台東区上野公園 2-1

dripping with water: it was discovered that at night they were sneaking down to Shinobazu Pond for a dip. This was considered improper behavior for shrine dragons, so wire cages were erected to keep them where they belonged. Poor little dragons, they long ago forgot the path and no longer need to be confined. They only get wet now when it rains. A small contribution allows you to walk through the shrine/museum and admire the almost too-pretty tea-house behind. You'll also see the newest replica of the old pagoda that dates back to 1639 in design if not in actuality.

Those who seek fulfillment in art galleries, museums, and zoos will find these places wherever fate puts them down. For such people, Ueno Park will provide hours of pleasure. There are many guidebooks and English-language identifications, so our comments will be few. Certainly the Tokyo National Museum (東京国立博物館), dominating the landscape at the end of the central reflecting pool and one of the world's great repositories of Oriental art, is a must on any art lover's list. And you should realize that those magnificent sculptures at the National Museum of Western Art (西洋美術館) are not copies but were cast from Rodin's original molds. Those and a large number of other art works are a part of the accumulation of Kojiro Matsukata, a wealthy art lover who assembled a fabulous collection in Europe in the early 20th century. His method of buying was distinctive and gave him great fame. He purchased by blocks: I'll take those six statues, the three over there, and all the paintings along that wall. . . .

The zoo? No one should miss the giant pandas, for no more appealing animal has ever been created. They were a gift from the Peking government. Also be sure to observe those who come to see the pandas. The last time I was there, a woman had brought along her own giant panda, a stuffed toy. She was carrying it ombu-style on her back, like a baby.

1. Ueno Seiyoken, 4–58 Ueno Koen, Taito-ku; tel. 821–2181
   上野精養軒　台東区上野公園 4–58

You don't have to pack a picnic for your visit to the park. Seiyoken,[1] Japan's oldest purveyor of Western foods (since 1873), is headquartered here in a three-story building with restaurants and party facilities. There are branches in the National Museum and in other places throughout the park. Seiyoken can also set up a yakitori or sushi stand at your next party if you'd like to create a Japanese environment.

In addition, there are many stands and lunchrooms along the pathways with a variety of Japanese and quasi-Western foods. If you want a novel experience, you can try the student restaurants at the Tokyo University of Arts. Two of them—those at the music school（音楽学部キャッスル）and the art school（美術学部大浦）—are open to the public and feature wholesome food at reasonable prices.

This should be enough to get you started on your own sightseeing route through Ueno Park, but there is always something else. Try to come here during the cherry-blossom season. You and some million or more others will be following one of Edo's early customs. If you forget your own bottle of sakè, friendly Japanese will surely invite you to join their party. Relax and have fun among the blossoms, for all too soon it (the word is left for your own interpretation) will fade away.

And I suppose you should know that the park was once a battlefield, for a useless final stand on the part of supporters of the last shogun, who had already surrendered his authority to those demanding the return of power to the emperor at the time of the Meiji Restoration. The battle was a gesture of gallantry with no chance of success. Rain was falling on that May day in 1868. Shinobazu Pond had overflowed and the battle was waged, for many, in waist-deep water. Descriptions sound picturesque—field guns set up in a cave-shrine dedicated to the fox god, cannon firing from the second floor of a restaurant-teahouse—but wars are romantic only in the retelling. Many men lost their lives and their dreams in the muddy marshes of Ueno. You'll see a statue of Takamori Saigo, one of the heroes of that day, who was fighting for the restoration, at the main entrance to the park. Later he was to lose his life in another rebellion. Then he was on the other side, opposing the policies of the government. Never mind, he is honored as one of the finest in the samurai tradition, courageous in adversity, magnanimous in victory.

Many of the historic buildings were destroyed during the battle of Ueno, among them the original Kan'ei-ji (寛永寺), head temple of the powerful Tendai sect, which once owned much of the land we now know as Ueno Park. To replace it, the present temple was brought from its former site in Gumma Prefecture. The Tokugawa shoguns worshiped here and a number of them are memorialized within the temple grounds.

We should note, I suppose, that, after being president of the United States, General Ulysses S. Grant and his wife came to Ueno Park during his 1879 visit to Japan and planted a couple of trees here. A monument was erected in his honor.

All this is at the back exit of Ueno Station, near the Yamanote tracks. There is also another Ueno with crowded streets filled with shops, restaurants, bars, coffeehouses, department stores, discount corners, cabarets, Turkish baths, theaters, hotels, pachinko parlors, fruit stands, and business offices all jumbled together along alleys, lanes, and thoroughfares. Or, in other words, a typical major station environment. Ueno, Tokyo's fourth largest station, handles more than a million people each day.

And if you follow the main street leading from the north side of the station toward the Asakusa amusement district (not on our Yamanote route, but worth many visits all the same; now covered in our second volume, *More Foot-loose in Tokyo*), you'll find shop after shop selling Buddhist altars, family shrines, and all the accounterments of Buddhist and Shinto worship. Buy yourself a small piece of altar furnishings as a memento of your Ueno visit—and your aching feet.

TOFU AND MORNING-GLORIES

Uguisudani: Nightingale Valley

NIGHTINGALES?—obviously a reference to a long-gone environment. The story goes that Kenzan Ogata, a famed 18th-century potter and painter, brought nightingales from Kyoto to present to the imperial prince who served as head of Rinno-ji temple. He released the birds in the wooded area north and west of the present station.

The Japanese nightingale (technically a kind of bush warbler) is regarded as the harbinger of spring and is greatly cherished for its sweet song. Noblemen kept uguisu in elaborate cages of polished bamboo with decorations of lacquer and ivory. Trainers were hired who could teach them to sing even more melodiously, and special

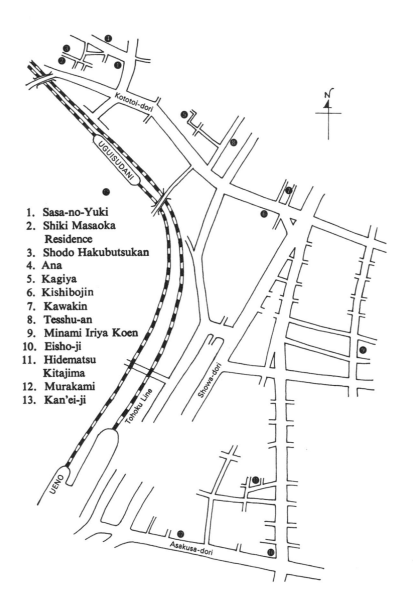

1. Sasa-no-Yuki
2. Shiki Masaoka
   Residence
3. Shodo Hakubutsukan
4. Ana
5. Kagiya
6. Kishibojin
7. Kawakin
8. Tesshu-an
9. Minami Iriya Koen
10. Eisho-ji
11. Hidematsu
    Kitajima
12. Murakami
13. Kan'ei-ji

attendants were assigned to their care. And in line with the modern concept of recycling, nightingale droppings were valued by the ladies. Mixed with warm water, they were used to bathe the face, or they could be put into a cloth bag along with nuka (rice bran) and used as a sponge in the bath. *Uguisu no fun* was reputed to do wonders for the complexion. You can still buy the droppings at old-style drugstores, and most bird stores also sell them, scooping up the desired amount in a traditional wooden-box measure.

From the north exit, cross Kototoi-dori for a restaurant that appeals to Edo-inclined Japanese as well as to modern health-food enthusiasts who seek out natural foods. This is Sasa-no-Yuki,[1] an old establishment rebuilt in classic style several years ago when the street was widened. It serves only tofu, a high protein Japanese staple made of soy beans. The restaurant name means "snow on bamboo," which is how the pure white tofu appeared to a visiting prince when he established one of the shop's traditions. He found the house specialty—tofu served in a sweet sauce—so delicious that he requested a second serving. Ever since that day, this particular dish is served in a double portion. Those less eclectic in their taste can have a tempura course to accompany the tofu if they place their order well in advance. There is a special lunch menu made up of five tofu dishes. (Test your chopstick skill with them: even the Japanese regard it as a sign of great dexterity if you can pick up one of the soft squares and pop it in your mouth without breaking it.) Prices are reasonable. For a few days every July the restaurant also serves a tofu breakfast from 5 a.m. This is during the morning-glory fair that you'll read about later in this chapter.

Well-fortified with your tofu meal, follow along Kototoi-dori. Just before the bridge on the right is the residence of Shiki Masaoka, a well-known haiku poet of Meiji times. The house has been rebuilt but follows the original design. Across the street is the Shodo

---

1. Sasa-no-Yuki, 2–15–10 Negishi, Taito-ku; tel. 873–1145
笹の雪　台東区根岸 2-15-10

Hakubutsukan, another house/museum, which displays the calligraphy of its famous Meiji-era artist-owner, Fusetsu Nakamura, along with his personal calligraphy collection.

Continuing back on the wide street going toward Sasa-no-Yuki, you will pass another famous restaurant, but whether or not you would like to try its specialty depends on individual preferences. Ana[2] features snake cookery.

Next, Kagiya,[3] typical of old-style Japanese pubs, or akachochin, so-named for the red lantern they all display in front. Open only in the evening, such neighborhood restaurants serve sakè (and more recently, whiskey) and specialties of the house that are considered to be good companions for drinking. And good companionship is what drinking is all about. At Kagiya's, it is a man's sport. Women alone are not admitted.

Kagiya has a history of over 125 years. Tired travelers for the shogunate stopped here for refreshment, samurai knew its menu well, and neighborhood residents stopped in to exchange gossip. If they should return to their old neighborhood, surely Kagiya would be one of the first places they would search for. They would find it a few blocks from the original location. The old sakaya stood in the way of progress, a street-widening project. When it relocated, it moved its furnishings as well, so you can still sit at the same time-worn bar or at one of the low tables on the scarred tatami-matted floor, spending only a few hundred yen for the evening's food, drink, and companionship.

Walking back toward the station, look for a temple dedicated to Kishibojin (鬼子母神), the child-protecting goddess whom we'll meet again in the Mejiro chapter. People come here to ask the gods to watch over their children's health and to protect them from mis-

2. Ana, 2–12–11 Negishi, Taito-ku; tel. 875–9155
   阿奈　台東区根岸 2-12-11
3. Kagiya, 3–6–23 Negishi, Taito-ku; tel. 872–2227
   鍵屋　台東区根岸 3-6-23

fortune. Its three-day morning-glory market—asagao ichi—held each year in early July draws thousands of visitors. The flowers, trained to grow on sticks in small pots, represent an astonishing number of varieties and colors. The festival continues a popular pastime of old Edo. The nobility raised bonsai, dwarf trees; the common people raised morning-glories, and the summer market, with villagers comparing unusual flowers and skillful arrangements, was a much-anticipated social event. In far earlier times, from the 9th century, the morning-glory was raised for its seeds, which were used as medicine. It was also valued for sentimental reasons. A famous poem translates: "Asagao taking hold of the well bucket, I ask a neighbor for water." Since morning-glories were entwined on the bucket's handle, the woman, not wishing to disturb the flowers, gets water from a neighbor.

The poem could be as appropriate today. As you look along the back streets lined with little houses and small entranceways, you will see a profusion of flowers and plants growing in all kinds of containers. In Japan you are never far from some greenery that catches, and soothes, your eyes. Nor are you ever very far from a place to eat. Nearby are two neighborhood restaurants worth noting—a branch of Kawakin, a popular Asakusa tonkatsu-ya (deep-fried-pork shop); and Tesshu-an,[4] a noodle shop once frequented by swordsman-calligrapher Tesshu Yamaoka. Well, not really *that* one: like Kagiya, the sakè shop, it has been relocated not once but several times. It may be hard to imagine what the original must have looked like when you see this rather dingy shop with its spotted, plastic-topped tables and cement floor, but look above the counter. There you will see a wooden sign of great value, the calligraphy of Tesshu, drawn one night long ago as he sat drinking sakè with the original proprietor. Finding a place to eat, often one

---

4. Tesshu-an, 3–2 Negishi, Taito-ku; tel. 874–3893
鉄舟庵　台東区根岸 3-2

with some claim to at least a minute place in history, is never a problem in any Japanese neighborhood.

Do you wonder about Japan's senior citizens? Walk toward Asakusa-dori. On the left will be a small park, Minami Iriya Koen (南入谷公園). There you'll find a number of venerable gentlemen reminiscing about the good old days. In the same way that Japanese seldom ask a child's age but rather what year he is in school, being able to guess his approximate age from his school year, these men identify themselves by telling what year they took their physical examination for military service at the age of twenty. (In the United States, a group of alumni from, say, Harvard might well follow a similar practice in saying they're "Class of '37" or "Class of '58.") But don't ask these old men to recommend a restaurant for lunch. They won't know; they all return home—their own, a daughter-in-law's—for their noon meal. They are not the lonesome, forgotten old men seen so often in parks in many other countries.

Next, turn right on Asakusa-dori to Eisho-ji (永昌寺), the temple where Jigoro Kano, a famous educator, founded his school of judo, the first Kodokan, in 1882. This Japanese martial art, whose name translates, roughly, as "the way of gentleness" or "the way of flexiblity," can be traced back at least three hundred years to ancient fighting arts of the samurai and even to Japanese sumo and Chinese "temple boxing." Using no weapons, it was certainly "gentle" when compared with sword fighting. It was Kano who gave judo its modern form—often called Kodokan judo—his big contribution being in advocating its use for self-defense only, eliminating the aspects that would kill or maim an opponent: with the abolition of the samurai class, such violence was considered to be no longer necessary. Kano also placed great emphasis on spiritual training, which he felt was essential for mastering the new judo. There were nine students in the first Kodokan, and two rooms, one of seven mats and one of twelve. Now judo is known throughout the world.

A few minutes' walk from Eisho-ji is the home workshop of

Hidematsu Kitajima,[5] a leader among the seventy-odd members of the woodblock-print association, an independent follower of old traditions. He accepts orders from admiring visitors, but only if he likes them. If your approach is correct, perhaps he'll do your Christmas cards.

If you are still hungry after your tofu, tonkatsu, noodles, and nibbles at the sign of the red lantern, you can stop at the Murakami,[6] a restaurant famous for its turtle cuisine. Lunch specials are rather inexpensive, but don't expect your evening feast to be a bargain.

Should you want to add more history to this stop, cross the tracks to the other side of the station. Here you will find Kan'ei-ji (寛永寺), a temple built by the Tokugawa shogunate, where several of the rulers are buried. The temple can be recognized by the large courtyard and the low, sturdy building with its high, sloping roof. There are three burial grounds nearby. Our station itineraries sometimes run together. You can also include Kan'ei-ji with your Ueno Station temple tour.

---

5. Hidematsu Kitajima, 5–12–9 Higashi Ueno, Taito-ku; tel. 841–3950
   北島秀松　台東区東上野 5–12–9
6. Murakami Suppon Hompo, 4–2–2 Higashi Ueno, Taito-ku; tel. 841–9831
   村上スッポン本舗　台東区東上野 4–2–2

14,000 JIZO

Nippori: Sunset Village

SUNSET VILLAGE? Some say it was given this name because a daimyo procession setting out in this direction from Edo would reach
Nippori late in the afternoon. Others say it was because the spot
was so beautiful that you wanted to stay enjoying the scenery till
sunset. Whatever the derivation of the name, today you reach Nippori on the Yamanote Line from Tokyo Station within ten or fifteen minutes and, once there, have to search hard for remnants
of the old beauty.

This may prove to be one of the most difficult stations to get
out of, a confusion of signs and steps. For easy exit, walk away

from the Uguisudani direction toward the end of the platform, go up the steps, and turn left. You will find yourself in one of the areas forming Edo's shitamachi, the downtown of earlier days, when life moved at a different pace.

Slightly to the left of the exit is a large map, a guide to points of interest in the area. Pass it by with a sigh. The language is Japanese. It often seems that the only signs posted in English near scenic or historic places tell us to keep off the grass or not to start fires within fifty meters.

If you could read the sign, however, you would learn that old shell mounds and outlines of ancient tombs indicate that people have lived here since the earliest days. In more recent times it was known for its cherry blossoms. Early woodblock prints show spring scenes, rolling hills covered with clouds of soft pink blossoms.

Walk up the steps behind the map and you will be in Yanaka Cemetery, one of Tokyo's four largest. The others are Somei near Sugamo Station, Aoyama not far from Roppongi, and Zoshigaya in Ikebukuro. Many people well known to the Japanese are buried here, men such as Taikan Yokoyama, the artist; Michio Miyagi, a blind koto player and composer; and Dr. Tomitaro Makino, an internationally known botanist. There is also a memorial for the destitute and unknown who were buried here after their unclaimed and unidentified bodies contributed to the education of medical students at Tokyo University.

The first temple you'll come upon is Tenno-ji (天王寺). It was here that the first government-approved lottery was held, in 1732. The top prize?—one hundred ryo. It's always hard to judge old values in today's terms, but the consensus seems to be that a hundred ryo would equal about five thousand dollars today. Now that would hardly be considered a great fortune, but then a hundred ryo's worth of rice could take care of a man for life, for rice was the standard measure of wealth. Even a daimyo's rank was determined by how many bushels his fief produced each year. As for governmental lotteries, they are still very much a part of the Japan

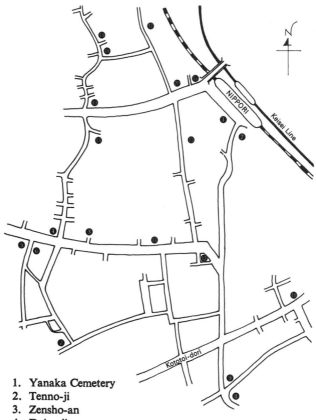

1. Yanaka Cemetery
2. Tenno-ji
3. Zensho-an
4. Daien-ji
5. Isetatsu
6. Chiga
7. Daimyo Clock Museum
8. Tokyo University of Arts
9. Torindo
10. Jomyo-in
11. Taguchi Ningyo-ten
12. Makino
13. Miyoji Buseki
14. Nihon Bijutsuin
15. Asakura Sculpture Hall
16. Hongyo-ji
17. Joko-ji
18. Shusei-in
19. Seiun-ji
20. Keio-ji

scene. They are held several times each month, and a top prize can run as high as a hundred thousand dollars or more, tax free. I'll leave it for the reader to figure out how much rice that would buy.

Once there was a tall pagoda in the center of the cemetery, made famous by a novel, *The Five-Storied Pagoda*, by Rohan Koda. It burned down in 1957, a funeral pyre, it was thought, of star-crossed lovers. Now only the site can be seen, and the flat stones that marked the four corners and the center of the building. They once provided a firm foundation for the wooden structure.

Stroll through the cemetery, enjoy the stillness, admire the moss-covered memorials and stone lanterns. Children play in the wide streets, businessmen take a shortcut to the station, housewives carry home their basket-packed purchases from nearby stores. You may see a family visiting a grave, and during the midsummer Obon Festival, when the spirits of the dead return to our world, perhaps a picnic as the ancestors on the "other shore" are brought up to date on family activities. Shed a tear for the dead and the past if you will, but remember that there is joy in continuation. A Japanese cemetery teaches this lesson well.

There are a number of temples on the other side of the cemetery, among them Zensho-an (全生庵). Here you will find the grave of Tetsutaro (Tesshu) Yamaoka, a famous swordsman, calligrapher, and supporter of Zen Buddhism during the Edo and Meiji periods. He served both the last shogun and, after the restoration, Emperor Meiji. The story is often told of how Tesshu once threw the emperor in a demonstration of sumo. It is obvious that the emperor thought well of him, since he remained a trusted court chamberlain even after this unusual demonstration of independence. (You may have seen an example of his calligraphy at the noodle shop on the Uguisudani itinerary.)

Another often-visited grave is that of the famous rakugo master named Encho. Rakugo is a combination of comic storytelling and pantomime. The storyteller sits on a cushion and, without any prop except his folding fan, tells familiar stories and acts out common situations. One famous turn that has held its popularity over the years is a demonstration—complete with sound—of soba eating. This is one of the few rakugo performances that are easily understood by foreigners.

Next, Daien-ji (大円寺). Here you will find a monument dedicated to Tokyo's first pin-up girl and the man who brought her fame some two hundred years ago. Beautiful Osen was a waitress at a small teashop that catered to those who visited Kutokurin-ji, a nearby temple. Harunobu chose her as his model for an ukiyoe (floating-world woodblock print), a decision that brought fame to both. Next to Osen's memorial is a Kannon statue surrounded by scrub brushes. It is thought that women can wash away various ailments by scrubbing the Buddha figure.

Look for a small shop, Isetatsu,[1] diagonally across the street from the temple. It sells a vast variety of delicate objects made of washi (handmade paper) in the style of Edo. Fans, boxes, chests of drawers, dolls, an endless collection of miniatures at inexpensive prices.

Around the corner, almost hidden behind its orange awning, is Chiga,[2] a tiny shop overflowing with well-designed folkcrafts. Look for the old-style folding wallets of hand-loomed cotton, for lacquer-lined bamboo spoons, for old-style folk toys. The shop name means "one thousand joys." Perhaps it describes the merchandise.

Daimyo—we're already familiar with this word meaning "feudal lord." But who thinks of these brave warriors checking their clocks for the time of day or battle? Today the world is well aware of the high quality of Japanese timepieces, and yet it's only the presentation that's new; in Edo days too the making of clocks was a highly developed skill. The Japanese sense of elegance is

1. Isetatsu, 2–18–9 Yanaka, Taito-ku; tel. 823–1453
   いせ辰　台東区谷中 2-18-9
2. Chiga, 2–9–11 Yanaka, Taito-ku; tel. 828–4179
   千賀　台東区谷中 2-9-11

apparent in the ancient devices that measured time by a path of burning incense. Also interesting are the clockfaces printed with both Japanese kanji and numerical symbols; the outer ring provided the names of the zodiac animals, essential if you were to keep in touch with these calendar signs that used to rule one's hours and days and years and life. For these and many more clocks and watches of Edo and Meiji days, some made in Japan and others imported from the West, visit the Museum of Daimyo Clocks.[3]

You will pass the Tokyo University of Arts (Tokyo Geijutsu Daigaku)—likely you'll recognize it from the practicing of many aspiring musicians—on your way to Torindo.[4] This old shop sells distinctive sweets—vegetables coated in white sugar—better known for their novel appearance than for their taste. They are a popular choice for gifts. You can buy a box of candied mixed vegetables for a thousand yen or so.

Jomyo-in (浄名院) is known for its many statues of Buddha, though Myoun Osho's dream has yet to be realized. He was the early priest who decided to solicit 84,000 statues of Jizo for his temple. There are now about 14,000, so if you would like to donate one, your gift will be welcome. One Jizo, holding a sponge gourd in his left hand, is considered to be a healing Buddha. His specialty, coughs and asthma. Because of Tokyo's air pollution and the consequent increase in the number of people with respiratory ailments, the temple is doing a rushing business, and grateful supplicants may yet help it reach its goal of 84,000 statues. For other ailments, visit the statue near the entrance. Again you'll find scrub brushes for washing away your pains. Remember to leave a small coin to assure successful treatment.

At the beginning of the Nippori story, we said that this area maintains much of the old downtown feeling from early Edo days.

3. Museum of Daimyo Clocks, 2–1–27 Yanaka, Taito-ku; tel. 821–6913
   大名時計博物館　台東区谷中 2–1–27
4. Torindo, 1–5–7 Ueno Sakuragi, Taito-ku; tel. 828–9826
   桃林堂　台東区上野桜木 1–5–7

Look in the shops as you walk along and you may see old trades being followed much as they were in the past. Perhaps you'll see an old woman bent over a charcoal fire toasting sembei. She'll brush one of the rice-flour crackers, still hot from the coals, with soy sauce and sell it to you if you ask.

A very special shop is Taguchi Ningyo-ten.[5] You'll see a surprising collection of doll heads in the window, some grotesque, some of early Edo beauties, along with miniature lanterns and firemen's standards, all made by Taguchi-san in his tiny shop. He and his seven apprentices travel throughout Japan taking orders. If you have visited any of the fall displays of chrysanthemum dolls, true-to-life figures enacting some famous historic scene, the heads might well have been made by Taguchi-san.

Especially attractive are the firemen's standards with their eye-catching decorations, always in black and white, bordered on the bottom with long strips of leather. In the days when the too-frequent fires were called the "flowers of Edo," every section of town had its own fire-fighting team, each vying for honors in this dangerous trade. Perhaps the most hazardous job was that of the standard bearer. Look! there he is!—standing on the top of the burning building holding aloft the standard, twirling and twisting it as he exhorts his colleagues to send up more water . . . because if they don't, they'll probably have to find a new standard bearer for the next fire. A much less dangerous job belonged to the men who stood on nearby buildings with huge fans. Their job: to direct the flames away from neighborhood structures.

At a busy intersection, look up to see a sign—in English!—advertising quite a different art, ivory carving. The name, Makino.[6] Step into the shop, threading your way past an assortment of tusks

5. Taguchi Ningyo-ten, 5-2-4 Yanaka, Taito-ku; tel. 821-3920
   田口人形店　台東区谷中 5-2-4
6. Makino Bros. and Co., 6-2-32 Yanaka, Taito-ku; tel. 821-4787
   牧野兄弟商会　台東区谷中 6-2-32

and teeth, admiring the carefully carved figures of birds and flowers, samurai, and basket weavers.

Basket weavers? You can see one at work. Walk down the hill and along the street that parallels the tracks. This was the main street in Edo days and your now-sharpened imagination will have little difficulty re-creating the pace of life of those times (though you may have to move fast to avoid today's traffic on the narrow lane). It's on this street that Miyoji Buseki[7] weaves his hanakago (flower baskets). He is one of the few craftsmen still working at this trade in Tokyo. Most of the baskets are made to order, and the few displaying price tags—one was marked ¥185,000—indicate that the craftsman's art is not unappreciated.

As you walk along, look for a small children's park. At this site, in 1887, Tenshin Okakura, art critic and author of books on the tea ceremony (including one in English, *The Book of Tea*), gathered other artists together to establish the Nihon Bijutsuin, an art school that helped launch many artists famous in Japan, among them Taikan Yokoyama. (Remember? Taikan's grave is in Yanaka Cemetery.) The school no longer exists, but a small hexagonal building enclosing a gilded bust of the founder marks the spot.

On the way back to the station, look for the Asakura Sculpture Hall,[8] which was formerly the studio-home of Fumio Asakura, a famous Japanese sculptor who died in 1964. The imposing, black-walled structure, with an impish figure surveying the scene from the roof, houses an extensive collection of his works. His love of bamboo is evident throughout the house. The roof-observatory provides an overall view of Nippori.

Back in the station area there are a number of other temples dedicated to the gentle pleasures—Hongyo-ji (本行寺) for moon view-

7. Buseki Hanakago-ten, 3–13–5 Nishi Nippori, Arakawa-ku; tel. 828–1746
　　武関花籠店　荒川区西口暮里 3-13 5
8. Asakura Choso-kan, 7–18–10 Yanaka, Taito-ku; tel. 821–4549
　　朝倉彫塑館　台東区谷中 7-18-10

ing, Joko-ji （浄光寺） for snow viewing, and Shusei-in （修性院） and
Seiun-ji （青雲寺） for cherry-blossom viewing. Reminders of less
gentle arts can be found at Keio-ji （経王寺）, where the gate is marred
by bullet holes from shots fired during the battle between the
last remaining group of shogunate supporters opposing the Meiji
Restoration.

The local citizens are aware of the historic significance of their
town within the city, and the Arakawa Ward Office has erected a
number of signs to mark the various spots of interest. For most of
us, they will make us wish once again that we could read Japanese.

You will surely have noticed the remarkably large number of
temples in the area. Here is one explanation. In the old days, temple
roofs were thatched. Consequently, they were easily ignited in the
frequent fires, and the winds blew the blazing straw to other buildings, making the fire much more difficult to contain. Finally, it was
ruled that temples should be roofed with tile. Ah, but this proved to
be no solution. The next disaster was an earthquake and the falling
tiles injured many people. Thatch was once again approved, but the
temples were moved here to the outskirts of the city. Needless to
say, it wasn't long before the ever-expanding city once again encom-
passed the temples. Apparently, earthquakes are now considered
less of a threat than fire. For years it has been illegal to construct a
new thatch roof within the city, so that only a few old ones (often
carefully repaired rather than being rethatched anew) now remain
here and there.

Nippori might appear to be an area of no interest as you speed by
on a train, yet it may prove to be one you'll return to often to
wander along the old streets, capturing the shitamachi mood. Your
travels will be better rewarded if you bring along a Japanese friend
who can translate the signs along the way.

PAPER DOLLS

Nishi Nippori: West Sunset Village

WE'D LIKE TO SUGGEST that you walk the short distance between Nippori and Nishi Nippori. It's not very far: you can see from one station to the other just down the tracks. You'll be traveling as people did in the old days, following the narrow, temple-lined road. Stop along the way, perhaps at a shrine called Suwa Jinja (諏訪神社), with its broad courtyard and adjoining cemetery. (The cemetery actually belongs to the temple next door: in most cases Japanese go to Shinto shrines for happy occasions, such as marriage or reporting the birth of a child, and to Buddhist temples for fun-

67

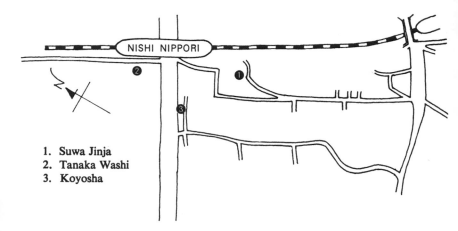

erals and burials.) This entire area was once so thickly wooded, it's said, that it was dark even in the daytime. Stand on the bluff and look across the tracks to the other part of Nippori—today's Japan, noisy, congested, a confusion of buildings and businesses. Yet it too can be picturesque, in its way, especially if you are an observer rather than a participator.

Nishi Nippori is an afterthought—a few places to visit near the station, and a cup of coffee—but perhaps a mini-tour is welcome after the extensive Nippori itinerary.

Cross the street just beyond the station and continue along the tracks. You'll come to a new building filled with modern shops. Only a short time ago this narrow street was lined with old family-owned stores, with the owners living over their shops. Most are now accommodated in one large modern building. The second floor (you can see the display windows from the train) has attracted mostly sporting-goods stores featuring skis, hiking boots, and swimming gear in proper season.

Even if you think you don't really care for paper dolls, you may discover you have some interest after all when you visit Tanaka

Washi,[1] a first-floor shop that specializes in the Japanese version that is far more than an amusement for little girls. The shop is lined floor to ceiling with shelves filled with sheets of washi (handmade paper) that later will be cut, folded, and shaped to create elaborately kimonoed dolls exactingly dressed in traditional styles. The papers are marvels to behold, some woodblock-printed with tiny, intricate patterns, others dyed, painted, or embossed. Not being bound by tradition, you can visualize these papers wrapping the special gifts you send home to favorite friends. You'll see teachers of dollmaking selecting just the right ones to be used by their students and, at the front of the store, examples of what skilled fingers can create from a few sheets of pretty paper. There are kits, too, everything you need for covering a miniature chest of drawers or a collection of boxes. These make appreciated gifts. And so does the paper. Even alone, it is a distinctive present.

You can continue on around the block and back to the main street, but be forewarned that it is a very large block. The high stone wall on your left is not the retaining wall for some splendid old mansion, though it might once have been. Now most mansions have been replaced by apartment buildings and prefab houses jammed together. You will see many of them if you take the high road back to the station. It comes out even with an overhead crosswalk.

On the other side of the street, at Koyosha,[3] you'll see a different kind of doll, the ones that are displayed in glass cases, often caught up in some action like dancing (girl dolls) or sword handling (boy dolls). The hundreds of dolls you'll find here are all the handiwork of one man. For accuracy, he copies the faces from old statues or paintings. Costumes and accessories, too, are historically correct in every detail. Almost hidden among the display shelves filled with

---

1. Tanaka Washi, 4–1–20 Nishi Nippori, Arakawa-ku; tel. 823–3710
   田中和紙　荒川区西日暮里 4-1-20
2. Koyosha, 3–6–13 Nishi Nippori, Arakawa-ku; tel. 821–7829
   紅陽社　荒川区西日暮里 3-6-13

dolls is a photograph that Nitobe-san, the proprietor, points to with pride. It was taken the day one of his dolls was presented to Princess Takamatsu.

Coffee shops are everywhere in Japan, though their locations and names change frequently. There was an especially nice one between the doll shop and the station when we toured Nishi Nippori. If it's not there now, another one likely will be, and it's a good time to stop for a little relaxation.

If you find yourself resenting the cost of coffee in Japan, remember that you are getting far more than a quick cup of this internationally popular beverage. Here each cup is individually brewed, with ceremony. At many shops you can even choose your favorite blend. Even more important, they provide a pleasant place for meeting friends. Offices are overcrowded in Japan; so are houses. The coffee shop has become the extension of the office, a substitute for the family living room. Remember too that there is no time limit, no feeling that others are waiting for your table, even though you ordered your cup of coffee an hour or so ago.

If after all this you still feel you are paying too much for such a tiny cup of coffee, order "American." The coffee is not quite as strong, but the cup is standard size and it's full!

There's one more thing about Nishi Nippori. You can think about it as you stand on the crowded train platform. Cranes were once a gourmet food in Japan, and crane soup was an epicurean delight. (For a restaurant whose founder was entrusted with preparing the cranes for the shogun's stew, see the chapter on Ningyocho in our *More Foot-loose in Tokyo*.) The finest cranes were found in the marshy Arakawa section just beyond the station. Cranes from Arakawa were presented to the shogun each year during the New Year celebrations, of which they soon became a part. The crane and the tortoise have long been symbols, both in China and Japan, of good luck and long life; there's even a saying to the effect that cranes live a thousand years and tortoises ten thousand.

田
場

AN INEXPENSIVE CURE

Tabata: Rice-Field Edge

HOW TIMES HAVE CHANGED since, as its name suggests, Tabata was in the paddy fields! To best see the difference, to view Tabata as it is today, look for the long blue iron bridge, Tabata Ohashi, to the right of the station. Below, a complex of tracks, evidence of the city's dependence on its rail system. Behind the station you'll see hills known as Dokan-yama and Asuka-yama. You probably know that *yama* means "mountain," and when you see these gentle rises you'll wonder how they could ever have claimed that name. But if you don't have a real mountain, you settle for a slope. The image is, after all, poetic. Early woodblock prints show them cov-

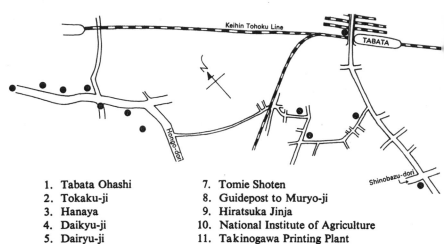

1. Tabata Ohashi
2. Tokaku-ji
3. Hanaya
4. Daikyu-ji
5. Dairyu-ji
6. Kyu Furukawa Garden
7. Tomie Shoten
8. Guidepost to Muryo-ji
9. Hiratsuka Jinja
10. National Institute of Agriculture
11. Takinogawa Printing Plant
12. Stone Marker

ered with cherry trees. Long ago, in the Sengoku period—in the 16th century when the Portuguese first reached Japan, when firearms were first being introduced, when the great families were still fighting to see who would rule the country—there were castles topping these yama, which proves, if nothing else, that they were the highest ground around. Today? Where the castles once stood there are coffee shops, cheap apartment houses, and love hotels—and a few mementos of the past.

Turn left from the station to reach the shopping area, passing along high stone walls. Look for a fish shop and then turn right. You'll soon be at Tokaku-ji (東覚寺), known for its Akagami Nio. Nio is the name given to the pair of fierce Deva kings who guard the gates of Buddhist temples.

Akagami. The word means "red paper," and the Nio statues wear quite a coating of them, a continuing collection since the local tradition was established around 1640. Go to the back of the compound, knock on the door of the house-office, and buy incense and red papers conveniently edged with paste. Place a bundle of incense (it is brought to you lighted) in front of each statue and paste the papers at an appropriate place. Suffering from gout? Paste a red paper on each obliging Nio's big toe and pass the pain on to them. Your small contribution for incense and paper makes it an inexpensive cure. Notice the collection of waraji (straw sandals) hanging near the statues. They are gifts from happy supplicants, cured of their illnesses. You don't find many waraji makers in Tokyo any more, so the temple orders them from Niigata. When you are sure of your cure, buy a pair for a few hundred yen at the office and leave them in appreciation, a small token of gratitude to the Nio.

If you are hungry, go back to the main street and windowshop your way to a large intersection. Cross the street, Shinobazu-dori, for Hanaya,[1] an old shop famous for preparing obento (boxed lunches). Order by the hundreds for a party or have lunch there, choosing from the models displayed in the window—osushi, tempura, or the typical lunchbox fare so familiar to the Japanese.

Actually, we've taken you too far. That large brick building down the street can also be seen from Komagome Station, next on our itinerary, so retrace your steps, noting the bargains compared to prices in your neighborhood. Notice too that many of the stores seem to have no doors to close. (Actually, there are solid shutters that are put up at close of business.) This is the old style. Once all stores were open-fronted even in the coldest weather. Then shopkeepers would catch a bit of warmth in their finger tips by holding them over the coals glowing in a hibachi. Now, with a gas or kerosene heater, they'll be warmer. Such stores can still be found throughout Japan, an invitation to all who pass by to stop in for a while.

Return to the street with the healing Nio. Walk along until you reach Daikyu-ji (大久寺), a secluded and sometimes quiet temple.

---

1. Hanaya, 4–40–3 Honkomagome, Bunkyo-ku; tel. 827–7575
花家　文京区本駒込 4–40–3

At other times, the stillness is pleasantly broken by the sounds of laughter from the yochien (kindergarten) next door. You'll find a stone protected by a strange three-legged canopy behind the temple. It is said that the famous priest Nichiren, wandering through Izu Peninsula, once rested beside this same stone. Later it was brought here. Perhaps you have seen pictures of Nichiren defying the Mongol invasion by calling on the kamikaze (divine wind) to rout the enemy. The Japanese remembered this same divine wind when they named their suicide pilots kamikaze during World War II.

Turn right at the main street shortly beyond, watching for a blue-and-white noren (curtain) above a gate on your right. This is the mark of a pawnshop, a shichiya. It's not really a shop. People visit the owner in his home to negotiate socially concerning the "loaning" of their goods. There are poignant stories of the numerous family crises that prompted the many trips a kimono would make to the pawnshop in the course of a lifetime.

Turn left at the next corner for Dairyu-ji (大竜寺). Walk up the hill behind the temple building. That imposing row of memorials marks the graves of temple priests. Just before you reach the top, to the right, is the grave of an American, Edward Howard House. The marker with the foreign name seems strange among the kanji inscriptions. House held an advisory position with the government in early Meiji days. Among his projects was the establishment of an English-language newspaper, the *Tokyo Times*, which supported the government position. The grave is well kept but bare, and I wished I had brought a flower. Perhaps one of you will.

Watch out for the trains! You'll be crossing one of the three remaining level crossings on the Yamanote Line. All three are to be replaced with overhead crossings, but the problems involved—cost and land acquisition—keep delaying the change. These mementos of the past won't be missed.

Look to your left for Komagome Station, next on our list. But, first, a stop at Kyu Furukawa Garden (旧古河庭園), a bit of old

English countryside in the heart of Tokyo. It was completed in 1917 by Baron Furukawa, a noted businessman during the early years of this century. The old English manor house was designed by Dr. Josiah Conder, professor of architecture at Tokyo Imperial University, who also supervised the construction of the Japanese Orthodox Cathedral, described in the Akihabara chapter. The entire garden was originally old English, but gradually it has taken on the color of the country and now it is a blend of English formality (in front of the mansion) and Japanese contrived naturalness (below the entrance). The grounds are beautifully maintained, but the house shows that it has been empty for years. During Occupation days, it provided what must have been surprisingly comfortable and familiar quarters. It was selected as being most appropriate for housing British officials.

Notice the roofs, all of copper. Furukawa was the name behind the Ashio copper mines. Copper from these mines contributed greatly to Japan's success in the Russo-Japanese War at the turn of the century. It also gave Japan its first case of industrial pollution, a countryside around the mines that even today is still dead, poisoned by copper wastes.

Walk toward the left when you leave the garden. Watch for Tomie Shoten, a small shop selling colorful mats, boxes, and other small treasures made of igusa, the same rush that is used to make tatami mats.

Look for an old-time stone marker in a narrow lane on the left, a guidepost to Muryo-ji temple on down that small street. Cross the wide street for Hiratsuka Jinja (平塚神社), a shrine named for the Hiratsuka Castle that once stood here. Pass by an old tree trunk, protected now by a copper roof (from Ashio?), a children's playground, and storehouses for the omikoshi (portable shrines) that are brought out for the local matsuri (festival) held twice a year, in mid-May and mid-September.

At the inner shrine, an old man removes the daily offerings of water, rice, and salt from in front of the altar. He tells us that on the first and fifteenth, the offerings also include a "mountain thing" (perhaps nuts or berries), a "ground thing" (some vegetables), and a "sea thing" (probably a fish). He points with pride to the fine paintings adorning the inner walls of the main building. Many depict the history of the Hiratsuka family.

There is a low mound with a bullet-shaped stone behind the shrine where a suit of Genji armor is said to be buried. The spirit of this armor was thought to be the family guardian. The gift was presented in 1083 at the time when the Genji clan was victorious in the northern campaign. The story is especially interesting since the Hiratsuka family claimed Heike descent. Later, the rivalry of these two great families, the Genji and the Heike, erupted into long years of conflict, but by then the armor's reputation had already been well established. Many romantic novels deal with this period. *The Heike Story*, a lyrical account of this conflict, is available in an excellent translation.

If you'd like to ponder all this, stop at the traditional teashop Hiratsuka-tei, to the right as you leave the shrine. No coffee here; instead, have toasted omochi (rice cake) wrapped in seaweed, or try the sweet drink, amazakè. Those soft lumps at the bottom are bits of the koji (yeast starter) used at the beginning of the sakè-making process. It's a pleasantly warming beverage on a chilly day. You can also choose sembei (rice crackers) or sweet bean cakes from the shop's display cases.

Continuing, you'll pass an open space that was once an agricultural institute. Now it is an emergency evacuation site and food storage area. Further along you'll see the Ministry of Finance's Takinogawa printing plant (大蔵省印刷局滝野川工場). If there are twenty or so people in your group, if you have phoned 910–1141 in advance to make an appointment, and if you have an interpreter, you are welcome to go inside to observe the process of stamp-making.

How could you miss that marker in the center of the road? The most obvious one warns drivers to be careful. Behind it, the recessed stone in the middle of the small park-like plot marks the distance from Nihon-bashi, eight kilometers or two ri, a ri equaling almost four kilometers or about 2.5 miles. Only two of these markers remain in today's Tokyo. The other is on Nakasendo (Hakusan-dori). In the old days, stone markers were to be found one ri apart on all highways. In addition to measuring distances, they functioned as early tax-meters. Charges for kago (palanquin) travel were levied by the ri. Passengers could count the markers to figure the proper fare. In those days too, late-night travelers probably paid higher fees; they couldn't see the markers in the dark and the carriers no doubt added on a few.

Sturdy hikers can retrace their steps, but by now most will welcome the idea of stopping a passing kago (sorry, taxi). If you are the two-station-a-day type, continue on a bit to the Honkomagome 1-chome Koban (police box), the most distant point described in our next tour; then you can follow the tour backwards to Komagome Station—and save the cost of a ticket between Tabata and Komagome!

EDO-STYLE GARDEN

Komagome: Horse Farms

KOMA IS an old Japanese word meaning "horse." That animal's history in Japan is long, extending back to the misty days of the mythological origins of the country. Japan's earliest chronicle reports that the Deity of Eight Thousand Spears "stood attired, with one august hand on the saddle of his august horse and one august foot in the august stirrup." The history of Komagome is far more recent, but even so it is difficult today to believe that this was once the area where horses were raised for the imperial court.

Leave from the west exit. Hongo-dori is directly in front of the station. In the old days, it was known as Iwatsuki-kaido, meaning the road to Iwatsuki, a town in Saitama Prefecture. It had another name: Onari-kaido, a road set aside for the exclusive use of the shogun. The designation was hardly necessary. Few people traveled in those days. Strict government regulations controlled residence. Farmers, for example, were forbidden to leave their land, to become tradesmen or craftsmen, or to allow strangers to stay in their villages. Only those who had been forced out of their niche in society were free to travel, if indeed *free* can be applied to those who had no home to leave and none to go to.

The first bridge you will see over the Yamanote tracks is Komagome-bashi. The second is known as Somei-bashi, named for a kind of cherry tree. Don't look for the trees now. They are only a memory preserved in a name. Perhaps it was the cherry trees that drew a special type of residents—the area was known for its flower growers, and especially those who raised chrysanthemums, the national flower of Japan. The skill of the artists who grew them was given international recognition by Breynius, the first European to mention chrysanthemums, in 1689. He called them *Matricaria japonica maxima.*

The area was also a storage place for lumber, and many large companies kept a ready supply here, for good reason. In case of a fire (and they were frequent) buildings had to be promptly rebuilt or the land would be confiscated by the government.

Going north from the station, you would soon reach Furukawa Garden, on the Tabata itinerary. Instead, go south. Scholars may choose to ignore the planned itinerary and spend their time at Toyo Bunko,[1] a research library reputed to have the city's largest selection of books, some 500,000, on Japan, China, and other Asian countries in English and other languages. The collection includes

1. Toyo Bunko, 2–28–21 Honkomagome, Bunkyo-ku; tel. 942–0121
東洋文庫　文京区本駒込 2-28-21

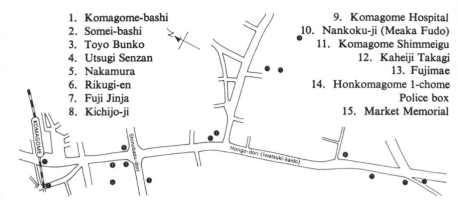

1. Komagome-bashi
2. Somei-bashi
3. Toyo Bunko
4. Utsugi Senzan
5. Nakamura
6. Rikugi-en
7. Fuji Jinja
8. Kichijo-ji

9. Komagome Hospital
10. Nankoku-ji (Meaka Fudo)
11. Komagome Shimmeigu
12. Kaheiji Takagi
13. Fujimae
14. Honkomagome 1-chome
    Police box
15. Market Memorial

early issues of periodicals dating back to the turn of the century. Since the library is mainly for those engaged in research projects, phone before you go to make the proper arrangements.

On the main street, watch for a tiny shop on the right owned by Utsugi Senzan,[2] a maker of stands, tiny treasures of wood, all lovingly created by hand. Admire the traditional tools along the wall, well worn by years of use. Small stands are available for a few thousand yen each, or you can have one made to order. Don't be in a hurry though. There are only a few stand makers in all of Tokyo. You must wait your turn.

If your interest is antiques, look for a store on the next corner, another across the street. Both have the same name: Nakamura.

Turn right at the corner for the entrance to Rikugi-en (六義園), a twenty-five-acre Edo-style garden that defies Tokyo's reputation as a city of concrete. It was created in 1702 by the feudal lord Yoshiyasu Yanagisawa, who was known for his literary accomplishments. The name itself suggests the six principles of composition for Oriental poems. The garden is in the Kwai-yu style. If you happen to be

2. Utsugi Senzan, 6–15–14 Honkomagome, Bunkyo-ku; tel. 946–4636
   宇都木栴山　文京区本駒込 6-15-14

knowledgeable in such matters, you will recognize eighty-eight spots along the pathways that commemorate familiar Chinese poems. In Meiji times, Yataro Iwasaki, a financial genius of those days, became the owner and restored the garden to its original perfection. He is better known as the founder of the Mitsubishi conglomerate. The garden remains today, an excellent and rare example of an Edo-style landscape art.

Returning to the main street, follow the wall that extends almost to Shinobazu-dori. About three hundred meters beyond this intersection, on the left, is Fuji Jinja （富士神社）. The shrine stands upon a mound that represents Mount Fuji. Once it was the center of a religion known as Fuji-ko, which held much appeal for the commoners of Edo. It was almost impossible to climb the sacred mountain in those days and this small hillock served as a substitute. The sect placed special emphasis on the Buddhist belief that what we do in our present existence determines our future lives and provides an explanation for our present sufferings—the results of ill-conceived actions in former lives. In 1849 the shogun promulgated the first of a number of restrictions prohibiting large gatherings of worshipers at the shrine, fearing that the seeds of revolt might be planted among the pliable people by misdirected leaders. Later, after the Meiji Restoration, the religion lost its appeal. For one thing, people could then climb the real Mount Fuji; they no longer felt any mystic power in the tiny replica. Today, the contrived hill overburdened with decorated stone memorial tablets is, for most visitors, only a curiosity.

Walk about a hundred meters straight ahead (you'll pass Komagome Shimmeigu, which we'll visit later in this chapter) to Hongo-dori. Turn left for Kichijo-ji temple （吉祥寺）, whose confusion of locations makes it difficult to chronicle or locate specifically. The original Kichijo-ji stood where the present Kikyo-mon gate of the palace now stands. It was built by Dokan Ota in 1457 to commemorate a fortuitous sign that emerged while he was building his Edo residence. Workmen dug up a gold piece marked with the symbol *kichijo* (good fortune) imprinted on it. Naturally, it was proper to erect a temple—Kichijo-ji—on the spot. In time it became one of the leading temples of the Soto sect of Zen Buddhism.

And in the meantime . . . In 1590, Ieyasu Tokugawa chose the land for his Edo castle and Kichijo-ji was moved to what is now Surugadai, the present site of Meiji and Chuo universities. It was destroyed in the great fire of 1657 and was rebuilt at its present location.

Temple treasures? Look for the kago (palanquin) in which the shogun was carried within the palace grounds, and the drum whose beat once announced the arrivals and departures of daimyo paying their respects at the shogun's court.

If you are wondering about the city Kichijoji on the Chuo Line, it has a related reason for its name. The people who lived near the temple were moved there after the big fire. You'll often find duplications of names, one in the city, another in the suburbs. There was no individual land ownership in those days, and the government often took over large areas after devastating fires. The plan was to use them as fire barriers, and the people who had lived there were moved to the suburbs. Soon, of course, the barrier area was filled again with wooden houses (Tokyo has always tended to abhor empty space) destined to go up in flames in the next fire as the cycle repeated itself.

See the tall building behind the temple? It's Komagome Hospital. Remember? You saw it from the corner when you had your obento lunch near Tabata Station.

Fudo, often called the Destroyer, is a Buddhist god with power to foil the snares of evil; his images often guard temples, showing a grim-faced deity surrounded by flames and carrying a sword for fighting demons and a rope for binding them. You'll find one of these images, called the Meaka (Red Eyes) Fudo, at Nankoku-ji (南谷寺), about a hundred meters farther along on the right. There are five of these "colored" Fudo in Tokyo. You'll meet another at Meguro (Black Eyes) and yet another at Mejiro (White Eyes). (And a Blue-eyed Fudo is said to have been set up in Yokohama shortly after Westerners, the "blue-eyed barbarians," began to live there.) The Fudo at Nankoku-ji doesn't rate having a station named for him, but he does have his own claim to distinction, having been christened by the shogun himself. The eighth Tokugawa shogun, Yoshimune, ordered his original name changed from Akame (Red Eyes)—derived from the fact that he was brought from Akame-yama in Kishu—to the reverse form so it would better match the names of the Fudo at Meguro and Mejiro. The small statue is inside the temple building. You'll have to request admittance at the door. And after all this, you'll discover that the little Fudo-san doesn't even have red eyes!

About a thousand meters beyond is a small shrine called Koma-gome Shimmeigu (駒込神明宮). It was rebuilt after the last war and isn't much to see, but note that the shrine (also called Tensho Jinja, dedicated to Amaterasu, the sun goddess) was already here by the year 1189—when the Western world was involved in the Crusades. Evidently, Komagome was a flourishing locality long before anyone had thought of Edo.

Turn left just before Komagome Shimmeigu and follow the narrow street to the end. There you will find a house that was reportedly built in 1716. Kaheiji Takagi, the original owner, was the nanushi (head man) of the village, a position the Takagi family had held since the Keicho era (1596–1615) when it was given permission to cultivate the lands around what is today Komagome. Descendants of the Takagi family are living in the house today. You'll be able to see only the wall and a marker, and the sweep of a tiled roof, but look again from the street that runs alongside for an idea of the estate behind the walls.

Back on the main street, contemplate on the changes that have occurred. Notice, for example, that many of the small businesses and shops now have office computers. It was only a few years ago that clerks checked the figures they obtained from their new electric cash registers on their soroban (abacus) to make certain they were correct. You must be aware, too, that the Japanese housewife is now mobile. If you are not, you are likely to be hit by one of the ubiquitous bicycles as you walk along. There is a lot of talk about bicycle lanes, but unfortunely there is no place to put them. And everywhere, modernization projects are engulfing the old places I send you out to see.

You will pass Fujimae,[1] a junk shop, the kind that challenges curious bargain hunters. Is the shop small, or is it packed so full that it only appears to be tiny? At any rate, no more than two or three customers can get inside at the same time.

Shortly beyond, across from Honkomagome 1-chome Police Box (本駒込一丁目交番), is a black stone marker at the entrance to a temple. It marks the site of an early vegetable market. Some 350 years ago people thronged here for their daily shopping. The small, winding street just beyond was once lined with teahouses where all kinds of amusements were available. Husbands probably slipped off in those early days for a game of chess or a cup of sakè in the company of a pretty waitress while wives shopped and gossiped.

1. Fujimae Bijutsu, 5-1-2 Honkomagome, Bunkyo-ku; tel. 945-5222
　　富士前美術　文京区本駒込 5-1-2

PAPER MEDICINE

Sugamo: Duck Nests

SUGAMO TAKES ITS NAME from its earlier rustic scenery. The written characters of the word mean "duck nests," reminding one of the ancient days when the land on which the station now stands consisted of marshes. The spoken word (though not the written one) could also stand for the sedge plants that once grew here in abundance. Either way, the Sugamo of an earlier day must have been inspiration for some of the country scenes that are so often seen decorating old screens. Ducks swimming about among water grasses have always been a popular subject for artists.

Now National Highway No. 17, Hakusan-dori, runs in front of

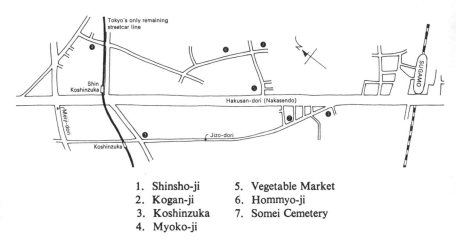

1. Shinsho-ji
2. Kogan-ji
3. Koshinzuka
4. Myoko-ji
5. Vegetable Market
6. Hommyo-ji
7. Somei Cemetery

the station. Today, as in Edo times, it is known as Nakasendo, one of the country's five main roads. Like the roads leading to Rome, these were first built for the convenience of the military. Their use was suddenly expanded in the 17th century when the "sankin kotai" system was established. It was this system that required daimyo to spend every other year in the capital, an effective method employed by the shogunate to prevent conspiracy in the provinces. It is estimated that each year as many as 146 daimyo processions used the Tokaido and 30 the Nakasendo (both connecting Edo with Kyoto), 37 the Oshu-kaido, 23 the Mito-kaido, and 3 the Koshu-kaido.

Of course a daimyo never traveled alone. He was expected to have a proper and splendid procession, often numbering several thousand persons, including samurai and servants—but not his legal wife. A daimyo's wife could not look forward to traveling with her husband. When he went back home she had to stay in the capital, a hostage to the shogun guaranteeing her husband's good behavior at home, at least politically. (Most daimyo found it convenient to maintain two complete households.) The watchword of the shogun's men at the checkpoints that examined passports along the highways was to guard against "women outward and guns inward" (that is, against conspirators' trying to get wives out of the capital or weapons into it). The system was most effective: not only did it help keep the Tokugawas in power for over 250 years, but it doubtless also created a demand for attractive daughters as wives or concubines either in the capital or back in the provinces.

Post towns or shukuba were established along these roads at intervals of every few miles to provide for the traveler's needs, whatever they might be. Some towns, favored by the shogun, were granted special privileges. The inns of Azuchi, for example, were assured of prosperity because of the shogun's regulation that required all merchants to spend at least one night there when they traveled along the Nakasendo.

The shukuba were also responsible for having horses ready for official messengers. For each horse there was a tax exemption of 30 to 40 tsubo of land. (The tsubo measure is still widely used in Japan today despite the metric system's now being compulsory; it equals about 36 square feet, being the equivalent of two of the tatami mats that cover the floor of a Japanese-style room.) There must have been many weary messengers stopping at Shinagawa for a final change of horses before their arrival at court. It is reported that the Shinagawa shukuba held 5,000 tsubo (slightly over 4 acres) of tax-exempt land—or around 150 horses.

Turn right as you leave the station. If you are hungry, explore the first small street. It is lined with a variety of Japanese-style restaurants, inexpensive lunches at noon and, at night, a gaudily lit entertainment section attracting commuters who need little encouragement to pause a while on their way home from work.

If you continue along the main street, Hakusan-dori, you will eventually reach Korakuen (amusement park, theaters, sports), Suidobashi (a nearby theater occasionally presents Noh dramas with English explanations), Jimbo-cho (old books), and finally the inner moat of the palace, but that's a different itinerary. Instead, cross the street when you reach the overpass. Walk a few steps back toward the station to the first corner. Turn to the right for Shinsho-ji (真性寺). In the courtyard you'll see a bronze statue of a Jizo wearing a farmer's hat. Six Jizo figures were cast between 1708 and 1720 and placed alongside the six major highways to protect travelers. (The sixth, not mentioned above, led to Chiba, not considered a destination of much importance.) All are sitting down, an unusual position for a Jizo, but one might assume that their responsibility tires them. The tradition of placing Jizo figures alongside roads continues. The unusual Noa building at Iikura 2-chome between the American Club and Tokyo Tower, a black shaft on a red sandstone base, has an alcove with a symbolic figure that the designer calls the Iikura Jizo, placed there to protect travelers at that busy intersection.

Back at the overpass, take the small street that branches off to the left. This is the old Nakasendo, commonly called Jizo-dori. You'll find the Jizo it is named for at Kogan-ji (高岩寺). His name is Toge-nuki, which means "splinter remover," but his fame has passed well beyond such a limited application. It is claimed that he can cure illnesses and solve problems. You can buy a packet of five tiny papers with line drawings of a Buddha figure at the temple—ask for *osugata*. It is claimed that if you swallow a paper, you will be cured, at least of the ailment you came with. To assure that the Jizo performs his magic effectively, the temple provides counseling service on Mondays, Wednesdays, and Fridays with professional people on hand to advise on such questions as children's education, inheritance problems, troubled marriages, and unrequited love.

Should a person want even more assurance of future well-being, there is also an image of Kannon, the goddess of mercy. Buy a brush and dipper and scrub down the statue to wash away your problems, if indeed you still have any after swallowing a curative paper and consulting the experts.

You will enjoy walking along the busy, narrow shopping street. It has often been rebuilt over the years, yet it still maintains much of the old-days atmosphere. There are stores selling Japanese candles (the prettily decorated ones with flowers are for funerals), bean-paste sweets, Chinese medicines, souvenirs, and daily necessities of all kinds.

Toward the end of the street, behind a wooden gate on the right, is a koshinzuka (庚申塚), a guidepost that once directed travelers along the old highway. Originally it stood three meters tall, but it was accidentally broken during the reconstruction work following the disastrous fire of 1657. The proprietor of the old tobacco shop across the street feels a responsibility for the ancient marker. His family has owned the property for the past three hundred years and he can weave quite a spell with stories of the old days, entwining his own memories with what he has heard of the past. Once his ancestors operated a teahouse at the busy corner and he recalls hearing how samurai often left valuable gifts in appreciation for the services provided.

Now you have a choice. You can catch a streetcar at the next intersection and ride to Otsuka, the next station. This is Tokyo's last old-style line, though a Setagaya line serves outer Shibuya.

Those of you who like to push on, who wonder what's around the next corner, can tour your way back to Sugamo Station. Cross the tracks and turn right on Meiji-dori. The road divides into three shortly after you cross Nakasendo. Take the right, and just before the bus depot you will be in an area of temples. One, Myoko-ji (妙行寺), contains several famous graves. For example, people interested in ghosts can search out the grave of Oiwa. Her haunting story is preserved in the Kabuki drama *Yotsuya Kaidan* (The Yotsuya Ghost Story). The grave is real; the story is fiction.

Ghost tales offered a sort of summer cooling system for residents of humid Edo. Frightening ghost shows and the telling of horror stories were popular entertainments, well attended for the chills they provided. Oiwa rates high on the cooling scale because of her dreadful face, horribly disfigured by the poison her husband, long-ing for his young mistress, forced her to drink. Naturally, the wife's ghost came back to haunt him. Although her spirit was eventually quieted, few can forget her terrifying face. In the old days, Oiwa's spirit was frequently called up to frighten small children (and perhaps straying husbands) into instant obedience. Even today there are some who do not wish to risk her wrath. Those taking the stage part of Oiwa—it's still a popular summer performance—make a special trip to the place where she did her haunting (in Yotsuya, where there's also a small shrine to her memory) to say a prayer for the peace of her soul.

The real Oiwa was a gentle woman with a devoted husband. Playwright Tsuruya Nanboku took her name and destroyed her reputation. And perhaps she is seeking vengence for that: Every theater that has been built in Yotsuya has soon burned to the ground. Some say it is because of Oiwa's angry ghost. More likely it is because she doesn't like the plot.

But let's get back to our itinerary. Myoko-ji has other attractions. Those who are sensitive to the spirits of the foods we consume can pay their respects at stone memorial markers, one for fish and one for eels, erected here by representatives of the Tsukiji fish market.

Return to the Nakasendo for a view of the Toshima branch of the central fruit and vegetable wholesale market. No retail sales—and no stone markers to commemorate the cabbages and onions.

The story of what was perhaps Edo's worst fire is told at our next stop, Hommyo-ji (本妙寺), a sad tale of three young girls brought successively to the temple for burial after sudden deaths. The priest realized, after the third, that all had been wearing the same kimono. It had been resold each time at the used-clothes mart. To put an end to the obviously cursed garment, he attempted to burn it in the temple grounds, but the flaming kimono leaped up and danced wildly among the buildings, catching them afire. The resultant catastrophe was known as the Great Furisode Fire, furisode being the name for the long-sleeved kimono the girls had worn.

Few accept this story as fact, suspecting that it may have been circulated to help hide a bit of carelessness on the part of temple officials who should have been more heedful when they built their fires. The conflagration did start at the temple. The date, January 18, 1657. The town gatekeeper in Asakusa heard that the prison in Demma-cho had opened its doors to allow prisoners to escape from the flames. Wanting to protect his people from these much-feared men, he closed and bolted his gates. Later, as the fire spread, fleeing residents were jammed against them. It is reported that ten thousand were burned to death trying to fight their way out of Asakusa. By nightfall of the first day, the fire had reached Nihon-bashi; the next day it spread to Kyobashi, Ginza, Shimbashi, and Kojimachi. It burned fiercely for two days and two nights. Then, on January 20, a great blizzard hit the still-smouldering city, and many of the survivors, with no way to keep warm, were frozen to death. More than 108,000 died during these ordeals of fire and ice. We refer often in this book to fires; this brief recounting can provide some understanding of the people's terror at the sound of the fire bell.

Perhaps appropriately, Somei, one of the four public cemeteries of Tokyo, is located behind the temple.

If you light a cigarette on your way back to the station, be certain that the match is out before you thow it away.

大塚

DON'T TOUCH!

Otsuka: Big Burial Mound

CHECK A MAP or guidebook and you might pass right on by Otsuka. There doesn't seem to be much of interest there. However—

Walk along the streetcar tracks—you'll hear more about streetcars later—to Tenso Jinja (天祖神社) on the left, a well-kept shrine in the classic style with two old trees tenaciously hanging on in spite of pollution and congestion. It is said that they are more than five hundred years old. Beneath one of the trees is a bulletin board with neighborhood announcements and a picture of how the shrine once looked: the reproduction of a woodblock print of cherry blossoms and open spaces.

Follow the tracks, passing good old C-58-407, a steam engine given a new home in a children's park. Unfortunately, children can't climb around on it. It's protected by a fence and they can only look.

Continue along the tracks, cross the main street, Kasuga-dori, and turn left. You'll pass a wholesale butcher (bargain prices, but there's a very good possibility that the ham you buy will taste of fish). The former fur store next door has gone out of business. Perhaps its stock was too limited in its appeal. Just how many people would buy a stuffed tanuki (Japanese badger) carrying a fishing pole, or his brother who held a golf club?

There are many small lumber dealers in the neighborhood, among them Kiyomatsu Ohno,[1] who deals in traditional woods, such as the corner posts that add distinction to the tokonoma, the recessed alcove in Japanese-style rooms where, in theory, treasures of the family are displayed. These days you may instead find the tokonoma filled with a color-television set and other consumer goods representative of today's affluence. You can buy, for $30 or so, a lovely length of bamboo forced to grow square by box-like wooden forms, or, for ten times that amount, a kind of post called shibori maruta, made of cedar that grows on the mountains near Kyoto. In the shop are many objects revealing the diverse interests of the Ohno family—fish raising, painting, and kite making. If you walk along the narrow street behind the store, you'll also see a roof full of the bonsai (dwarf trees) they raise. Should your visit be in May or June, you'll find them in impressive bloom. The family favorite is satsuki, a kind of azalea, which blossoms then.

Not long ago, walking along this street, you would have been surrounded by rice paddies. There are many people who remember. You may not be able to hear what Usami-san is saying because of the loudspeaker truck going by, but he'll tell you that when he

1. Ohno Meiboku-ten, 5–46–1 Higashi Ikebukuro, Toshima-ku; tel. 971–0673
大野銘木店　豊島区東池袋 5–46–1

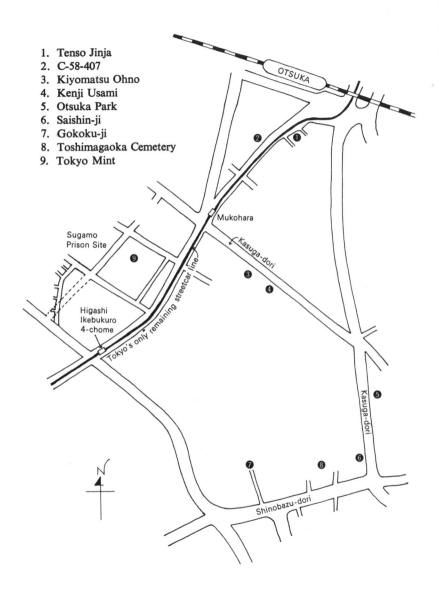

1. Tenso Jinja
2. C-58-407
3. Kiyomatsu Ohno
4. Kenji Usami
5. Otsuka Park
6. Saishin-ji
7. Gokoku-ji
8. Toshimagaoka Cemetery
9. Tokyo Mint

OTSUKA

Mukohara

Kasuga-dori

Sugamo
Prison Site

Tokyo's only remaining streetcar line

Higashi
Ikebukuro
4-chome

Kasuga-dori

Shinobazu-dori

N

opened his store sixty years ago, his customers were the neighborhood farmers to whom he sold his handmade tabi (mitten-like socks). You'll still find work clothes at his small shop,[2] but most of them are sold to the laborers who now live in the area. Yet, he tells us, there are farmers still working their fields not far beyond Ikebukuro Station, and they often come to buy their work tabi and their mompe (women's bloomer-like work pants) at his store. These too have changed. Modern ones have zipper pockets, a postwar innovation.

Continue on to Otsuka Park (大塚公園) on the left, once the estate of the Meiji financial expert Viscount Shibusawa, who helped make big business "respectable" after years of samurai disdain for commerce. The stone figures just inside the entrance once lined the road approaching what for many was the last stop, Sugamo Prison, whose formidable red brick walls reached almost as far as this small park. Then the old hospital across the street treated prison patients, and it still cares for the destitute. You'll read more of Sugamo Prison at the end of this chapter.

Turn left on leaving the park and stop just beyond its border at an old building with a narrow, shaded entranceway. You'll see an old stone kura (storehouse) at the back, and will perhaps wonder at the reason for the Russian-script decorations at the gate. There is a simple but rather surprising explanation. This was once a prospering pawnshop. The proprietor was offering a cover for his customers. Many were embarrassed to be seen entering such an establishment. Foreign language signs somehow seemed to provide an alternate reason for stopping in.

The present owner almost sold the land a few years ago, but then decided to keep it for his children, no matter that the children have interests other than pawnbrokerage. Now he and his wife continue

2. Kenji Usami, 5–50–8 Higashi Ikebukuro, Toshima-ku; tel. 982–2784
宇佐美賢次　豊島区東池袋 5-50-8

the old business on a very modest scale in an office lined with beautiful keyaki wood, its smooth glow a patina of age, not polish. The tree from which the walls and cabinets are made once stood in a shrine courtyard. The shopowner bought it when the shrine was about to be leveled to make way for a street-widening project.

He would suggest that you come to this area on a winter's night and stand at the line dividing his land from that of the garden. Watch the moon rise from behind his kura and you will see a bit of Tokyo exactly as it appeared in Meiji times. "In winter when the air is clear and the nights are still, it's not hard to imagine things as they once were," he says. He treasures keepsakes of those days. On the walls of his office are framed pages from old ledger books, remembrances of neighborhood transactions: a roll of white silk, 2 yen; a wool work kimono, 1 yen 20 sen; an eighteen-karat gold watch, 3 yen 50 sen.

Cross the street at the next intersection. Notice the temple slightly to the left, Saishin-ji (西信寺). Once a corner of the cemetery was set aside for the burial of dogs and cats. The old building beside the temple? It houses the offices of the Sato Detective Agency, one of Tokyo's oldest, often pictured on television.

Our destination, Gokoku-ji (護国寺), is one of Tokyo's largest temples. Many members of the imperial family are buried at the spacious and quiet Toshimagaoka Cemetery next to the temple. You will pass the firmly barred cemetery gates, but only visitors with special permission are allowed inside.

The temple is reached by climbing a flight of steps topped by a red gate. The large wooden structure to the left is the oldest building in Tokyo, though it is not a native. It was brought piece by piece from Otsu in 1887 and rebuilt in Shinagawa. In 1928 it was moved to its present location. Dating back to the Muromachi period, it is said to be around five hundred years old. The hondo (main building), built in 1697, was once about the size of the bell tower you'll see on the right. Favored by the mother of Tsunayoshi, the fifth shogun, it was enlarged to please her. Inside, to the right of the altar, you can see the palanquin in which she was carried when she visited the temple. The chief image enshrined here is a small Kannon made of amber that was brought from China. It is rarely put on public display.

Heading back toward the station, you will see one of Tokyo's four largest public cemeteries, Zoshigaya. Lafcadio Hearn is buried here. Continue on to the Zoheikyoku Tokyo Shikyoku (造幣局東京支局), the Tokyo branch of the government mint. The main office is in Osaka and another branch is located in Hiroshima. Five and ten yen coins are made here, and only a few years ago, ¥50 and ¥100 coins as well, but manufacture of the larger coins has been stopped because of anti-pollution and noise campaigns by the people who live in the nearby apartment houses. If you would like to go inside, call in advance to make arrangements—987-3131, extension 207, in Japanese. You will be able to see only a small part of the manufacturing process, including the stamping of the design on the coins, but you can linger over the displays—there's one of old coins—in the exhibition room.

Just beyond looms Tokyo's tallest building, Sunshine 60. A lonesome landmark, it is part of a dream to make Ikebukuro into a new city center. This was once the site of Sugamo Prison, which already had a long history when it was chosen to house the prisoners being tried for war crimes after World War II, among them the former prime minister and general, Hideki Tojo. Records are confusing about many of the trials and sentences although the stories of the top seven are well known. They were executed at midnight, two days before Christmas, in 1948. The execution grounds have been made into a small park. Of the other prisoners, it is reported that more than five thousand convictions were made, although some were multiple charges against the same person, and about three thousand sentences were pronounced. If you wait long enough to visit the site, you will find a huge complex of offices and shops, a new center for Ikebukuro with skyscrapers as high as forty stories. At least that's the plan.

Now you can return to Otsuka Station, or go to Ikebukuro, somewhat closer, and our next stop. You'll be able to relax when you get there—at a new style neighborhood bathhouse.

FRIENDLY MEETING

Ikebukuro: Bag Pond

IN THE OLD DAYS there was a pond somewhere near here. It was shaped like a bag, they say, and thus the district received its name, *ike* for "pond" and *bukuro* for "bag."

But there's much more to Ikebukuro than its name; next to Shinjuku, it's probably the busiest of Tokyo's outlying "cities." Study of a detailed map shows such diverse landmarks as a post office, a service center for the Tokyo Electric Power Company, and a railway training school. A corner marked Peace turns out to be the site of a tonkatsu (pork cutlet) restaurant.

But you discover more when you explore. Ikebukuro can be rec-

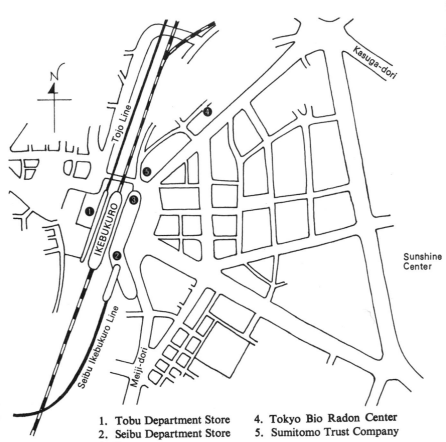

1. Tobu Department Store
2. Seibu Department Store
3. Parco
4. Tokyo Bio Radon Center
5. Sumitomo Trust Company

ommended to the no-expense-account crowd as a place to find entertainment at prices far more reasonable than the restaurants, night clubs, bars, coffee shops, and Turkish baths in other sections of town. Since Ikebukuro still draws a large number of country-type people, you will also find an attitude quite different from many other parts of our city: friendly, curious, and often of a quality that can be described best as earthy, though I hasten to add that this is by no means limited to Ikebukuro.

Adjoining the station on one side is Tobu, a monstrous department store, auditorium, amusement center, and office-building combine, and on the other, the main Seibu Department Store, which at this moment claims to have the largest floor space of any department store in Japan. Next to Seibu and merged with the station is Parco, a familiar accompaniment of Seibu stores, an eight-floor shopping center with boutiques and specialty shops stocking such goods as accessories, folkcrafts, novelties, records, imports, and posters, all topped with two floors of restaurants where you will find a decision-defying choice of foods, all attractively served in restaurants designed according to traditional concepts and at prices less shocking than usual. Exploring such buildings floor by floor is itself an education and you will learn a great deal about the preferences and habits of Japanese people. Crossing the main thoroughfare and investigating the bar-and-restaurant-lined streets beyond will be even more educational and less expensive, an accommodation to the many students who find their fun in the area, as well as to the rural population that looks to Ikebukuro as its shopping center.

No one should ignore the role of the bath in Japan. It involves far more than merely getting clean. It is a ceremony, a rite, an amusement. Public bathhouses are a necessity in a country that so greatly appreciates this water ritual yet fails to provide a large percentage of its dwellings with the required facilities. It was not only in Edo days that the bathhouse played its part as a social center of the neighborhood. Today, too, many bathhouses serve also as community meeting halls. Among these, Ikebukuro once had something very special indeed.

The Ikebukuro Onsen was typical, one bath for men, one for women, as is standard now except in a few resort areas where mixed bathing still prevails. The fee included a tiny towel (tenugui) that serves as both washcloth and towel, and provides a token of modesty. But never mind, in the bath, people look without seeing (or is it see without looking?). There were several types of baths, some bubbling from pressurized water, others claiming curative powers for almost any ailment. For those who are not familiar with Japan's bathing customs, it must be stressed that all washing and rinsing are done before entering the tub.

None of this was unusual, but still the Ikebukuro Onsen was unique. It had become the gathering place for a lot of old folks from all over Tokyo. Many stayed all day. After their bath, they would put on yukata (a cotton kimono) and go to the third floor. There, sitting at low tables on the tatami floor, they would order house specialties and share delicacies they had brought from home. But the best part was the informal entertainment. Anyone could perform on stage, singing or dancing, drawing caricatures or telling comic stories. Each was assured of the praise of their companions. Many had been professional performers in their younger days; for them, this was perhaps the only place where they could once again enjoy the spotlight and the applause that they once knew well.

That bath is gone now, but, as usual, there is something similar to replace it, the Tokyo Bio Radon Center.[1] The women's bath is on the second floor, the men's on the third, and on the fourth, there are small "family baths," party rooms, a restaurant, and, like the old days, a large tatami room with a stage for impromptu performances. If you have your own act, you can be sure of an appreciative audience. But its feature is radon gas.

Here one is issued a yukata, a tenugui, *and* a bath towel, but in the friendly ambiance of shared bathing, modesty is soon forgotten. First one scrubs and rinses (the house provides soap, shampoo, rinses, combs, brushes and hair dryers). Next, a refreshing pressure bath. Hold on to the metal guard rails and let the water

1. Tokyo Bio Radon Center 1–39–11 Higashi Ikebukuro; Toshima-ku; tel. 981–2441
東京バイオ・ラドン・センター　豊島区東池袋 1-39-11

jets massage the aches and pains in backs, shoulders, feet. Then move on to the radon bath, a glass-enclosed room where the gas bubbles up through the water. You will feel it at once, a warmth that opens your pores to spill out perspiration, leaving your skin tingling and refreshed. Ten minutes in the air bath is suggested before entering the tub. (The bath is not recommended for pregnant women.)

Then repeat the process as often as you like until you are tingly clean. There are resting rooms outside the bath enclosure where people gather to talk, watch TV, or simply relax. Then most will adjust their yukata and go to the special rooms upstairs for conversation and refreshments. Almost like the old days.

The owner, Masao Koshibe, studied in the U.S., specializing in ways to relieve stress. He found a sure cure in radon baths, which are well known in Europe and especially the Soviet Union where there are more than 1,000. Now he has a chain of radon baths in Japan and would like to introduce them in the U.S. The first one will likely be in Texas. He speaks English well, and will reassure you if you have any questions before exploring the healthful cleansing of a radon bath. Many health-oriented products are on sale at the front desk—massage sandals that soothe tired feet, do-it-yourself moxabustion kits, and herbal medicines.

One note of warning. Unless you are comfortable in crowds, avoid Saturdays, Sundays, and holidays.

You'll see a branch of the Sumitomo Trust and Banking Company on a corner near the bathhouse. It recently celebrated its twentieth anniversary. In honor of the occasion, employees spent their weekend cleaning up the neighborhood. Young executives, perched a bit awkwardly on stepladders, swept down, washed, and sometimes painted walls that appeared to have been collecting dirt since the day the bank first opened its doors. Assisting them, filling the buckets and collecting the trash, were pretty office girls with, for once, their hair in disarray and their faces dirty. I wondered if there are many places where employees would help mark their company's anniversary by giving their weekend to work that is viewed quite distastefully in Japan, where outside and inside dirt are considered quite differently, and almost no civic responsibility is felt for other people's litter, or even one's own.

Today, the showplace of Ikebukuro is Sunshine Center. Sunshine 60 dominates the skyline, at 60 stories the tallest building in Japan. People come from all over the country to marvel at its height, visiting the museum, the aquarium, and the spectacular laser show, an imaginative display of lights and images flashing over the theater ceiling as you sit, blessedly relaxed, in a reclining seat. At other times, the room becomes a computerized planetarium. A world trade center offers exhibitions and sales of foreign products, and a branch of Mitsukoshi competes with the seemingly endless boutiques, which feature every imaginable type of merchandise. If you want to stay awhile, there is a hotel in the same complex. A popular attraction is a fountain that responds to noise. Children clap their hands, shout, and stamp their feet, delighting in the changing patterns of the water.

Sunshine Center is now a four-building complex linked together with Alpa, a four-story shopping/restaurant complex. Alpa? It stands for Alpha, the first, number one. It is all part of a dream to make Ikebukuro a center for international activity. A start has been made. A number of countries, among them the United States, Canada, and ASEAN nations, have trade offices there. There is also an immigration center and a World Tourist Clinic. Foreign visitors may note a distressing lack of English information, but persevere, and you will find what you want. Or, if not, likely you will discover something of equal interest.

Remember, this was once the site of Sugamo Prison (see Otsuka chapter), but there are no ghosts. One can visualize haunted castles but never a haunted highrise. What ghost could find a comfortable haven among the polished corridors or chrome and plastic escalators, in the brightly-lighted display rooms or contemporary offices? Sugamo Prison is forgotten as Ikebukuro seeks a new image.

目白

PAMPAS-GRASS OWLS

Mejiro: White Eyes

THE NAME MEJIRO commemorates another of the Fudo images, this one called the White-eyed Fudo.

Turn right as you leave the station and soon you will be at the gates of the Gakushuin, once an exclusive school for children of the nobility but now open to all students who can pass the tough entrance examinations. Until 1950, the extensive campus was for junior and senior high-school boys. When Occupation authorities ordered the expansion of the higher education system after the war, a university was added and it was opened to girls.

If you care to explore the grounds, study the picture map at the

1. Gakushuin
2. Yoshioka
3. Earthquake Memorial
4. Shin Hase-dera (Mejiro Fudo)
5. Short street
6. Chinzan-so
7. Tokyo Cathedral
8. Kishibojin
9. International Catholic Hospital
10. Yakuo-in
11. Otomeyama Shizen Koen

entrance. Look friendly, and you may find yourself with a student guide who would like to practice English conversation. If you walk through the grounds to the next gate, you'll pass by several old Meiji-type buildings that once provided housing for some of the school's distinguished teachers. The headmaster's house has been moved to Meiji-mura, the park near Nagoya that exhibits (and protects) striking examples of Meiji architecture. The house at the open-air museum is in far better condition than those that remain on the campus.

Back on the main street, just beyond the university, is Yoshioka, a small shop selling imaginative craft goods made of igusa, the grass that's used to make tatami, and pottery brought in from the Okayama area. Igusa slippers are cool and comfortable in the summer, and the small-size woven mats in bright solid colors contribute to attractive table settings.

Notice the weathered wooden houses as you walk along, although they probably look older than they actually are. The jutting angles of the doorways sheltered by minute entrance gardens and old-style lighting fixtures with etched-glass shades are reminiscent of Meiji times.

Pass over a bridge, looking down at the highway below. Note the monument on the other side, a tribute to the man who planned the reconstruction of this part of Tokyo after the disastrous 1923 earthquake, and to the men who did the work.

Now, down the steps for the next in our collection of colored-eyed Fudo. You'll cross some streetcar tracks. Catch a streetcar here for Waseda University if you wish to specialize in campuses. Mejiro Fudo is a small figure sitting in front of his temple home, Shin Hase-dera (新長谷寺). Look closely. Is there a hint of white that might once have colored the eyes? With these Fudo, the color seems to be only in the name.

Back on Mejiro-dori, explore the short street on the right. In this small block you can take lessons in tea ceremony, traditional dances, and calligraphy, for the old-style Japanese houses behind the attractive gates and well-disciplined entrance gardens are also schools.

If you wish, you can go along Mejiro-dori to Chinzan-so,[1] a garden restaurant on an old estate previously owned by Aritomo Yamagata, a powerful leader during the Meiji Restoration who is remembered as the founder of the modern Japanese army. Now the

1. Chinzan-so, 2–10–8 Sekiguchi, Bunkyo-ku; tel. 943–1111
椿山荘　文京区関口 2-10-8

estate belongs to Fujita Travel Service. It is especially appealing on summer evenings when fireflies are brought in from the country and set free among the trees. Guests wander along the paths marveling at the flickering lights and remembering when the viewing of fireflies was possible in just about any area of the city. Today they must be imported. Some two million are flown in each year to re-create this old Tokyo diversion.

Across the street, an inspiration in concrete and steel, is the beautiful Tokyo Cathedral, designed by Kenzo Tange. We'll also see his soaring Olympic buildings near Harajuku Station.

If you cross Mejiro-dori and proceed straight ahead after leaving the White-eyed Fudo, you will find a temple dedicated to Kishibojin (鬼子母神), originally a female Hindu deity devoted to the protection of children. She wasn't always. In fact, she once took pleasure in devouring them. Finally she was reformed. The Buddha came to her and asked how she'd like it if someone ate *her* children. She realized the error of her ways and has been watching over children ever since. You will see many reproductions—pictures, carvings, and emblems—of pomegranates. Supposedly Buddha told the goddess to satisfy her hunger with this fruit instead of children. It is interesting to note that pomegranates are symbolic of fertility.

To the right of the main building is a carving of Kishibojin that was found, they say, in a neighboring rice paddy in 1561. Some 150 years later, in 1707, a shrine was built to shelter it.

There are two other statues preserved at this temple: large-sized Nio, gate guardians, that were carved, according to a date engraved on the base, in 1691. Perhaps they will be decorated with bright squares of paper that have been pasted on them. Some people believe they can get rid of any illness by symbolically presenting it to the Nio (see Tabata chapter).

On October 18 the temple holds a spectacular lantern procession. Little owls made of pampas grass, famous throughout Japan, are sold then. There are only a few people who still make these appealing little figures, and the pampas grass used to make them becomes more scarce each year. The price? It goes up, of course. The little owls may soon be coveted treasures instead of amusing novelties.

The small street behind the temple is worth exploring if you enjoy walking along old shopping areas typical of Tokyo's past.

Had you proceeded in the opposite direction from the station, you would have reached another landmark of the area, one well known to many foreign residents of Tokyo, but we have no intention of including it on our joy-filled tour of Tokyo. It is the International Catholic Hospital, known also as Seibo Byoin.

We suggest, however, that garden lovers (and even garden tolerators) start out in that direction. There are two delightful garden stops along the way.

The peony has been selected by many artists of the East for picturing in paintings, porcelain, and lacquer. If you should visit Yakuo-in temple (薬王院) with its Botan-en (Peony Garden) in May, you will know why. The vivid colors, the delicate turn of a petal, the contrast of the sturdy leaves, make Botan-en more of an experience than a garden.

Quite in contrast, yet with its own special appeal, is Otomeyama Shizen Koen (乙女山自然公園). The word *shizen* means "natural." You will find it used when you go shopping for health foods at "shizen" stores. Applied to a garden, it means that it has been left in a natural state, appearing as if it were untouched (and hopefully uncluttered) by man.

The name is appropriate. The park should have a special marker commemorating it for the ages. A few years ago, what was perhaps Tokyo's first ecology battle was waged here. The area was slated to become a huge apartment development, and the neighborhood banded together in opposition. They couldn't save it all—look for the neighboring apartment buildings—but they managed to save some. Now, walking along the wooded paths, listening to the sound of flowing water, and savoring the quiet, it is hard to believe that the city is so close. The grounds were once a daimyo's garden. One suspects that he is pleased. While he may have opposed uprisings by the people in the past, he would surely approve of the results of united action by today's citizens in objecting to high-rises in his garden.

A BACKWARD GLANCE

Takadanobaba: Upper-Rice-Field Riding Grounds

YES, AND VESTIGES of the old riding grounds yet remain. Let's set out in search of them, walking along Waseda-dori. Follow the street a bit further than we'll take you and you'll find Waseda University, one of the country's most prestigious private universities and one of the few with classes in English for foreign students, a program established to meet the growing demands of undergraduates who want a year of study abroad. Theater lovers should visit the Tsubouchi Memorial Theater at Waseda, the only stage museum in Japan.

Look for Big Box next to the station. Big Box is a building,

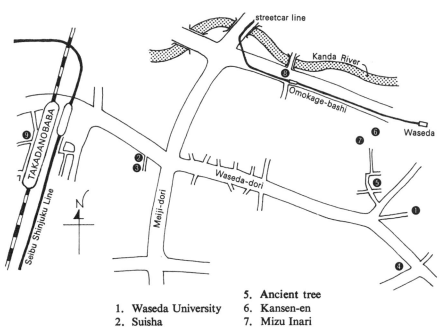

1. Waseda University
2. Suisha
3. Irori
4. Ana Hachiman
5. Ancient tree
6. Kansen-en
7. Mizu Inari
8. Omokage-bashi
9. Suzuya

its large, covered entranceway typical of any student-oriented area. It is designed for books and browsing. The first two floors are given over to small shops and restaurants, but after that, it gets down to its real business, physical fitness and sports. There are many sports clubs in Tokyo with a variety of facilities, some featuring such specialized equipment as deep diving tanks and indoor ski runs. Big Box is less dramatic. It is reasonably priced to accomodate its mainly-student clientele. You can swim, play pool, exercise, practice golf or tennis, bowl, and listen to hi-fi music, all within the confines of Big Box.

Reasonably priced restaurants, coffee shops, and bars line the streets. If you are an evening traveler, and would like a different dining experience, two after-five restaurants may attract you with their folksy-craftsy décors. First you'll see Suisha (Waterwheel); next to it, around the corner, is Irori, the word for the open hearths used in the old days for cooking. The first serves okonomiyaki, a Japanese do-it-yourself pancake. The batter is served in a cup along with mixed vegetables and your choice of seafood (shrimp or squid) or meat (beef or pork) with a raw quail's egg on top. Mix as you like and fry on the griddle built into the table in front of you. It's a popular and traditional dish that is more common in Kyoto than Tokyo. The Irori is a country-kitchen restaurant that displays the foods served on woven basket-like plates. Point to what you want and it will be grilled especially for you. Prices are reasonable, the atmosphere is relaxed and friendly.

You'll realize it's a student-oriented neighborhood if you pause to look in the windows of the photo shops. You'll see pictures of students in caps and gowns, in hakama and haori, alone and in family portraits.

Continue on till you reach the steps that lead up to Ana Hachiman (穴八幡) Shrine. *Ana* means "hole," but no one can say now what the hole commemorates, or where the hole (if indeed there was one) was located. Today Ana Hachiman is a favorite of families. At any season of the year you will find mothers and children enjoying the wide expanse in front of the shrine. The high elevation provides a fine view of the city below, especially if you are looking through cherry blossoms or fall leaves.

Now retrace your steps and cross the street. The wooded area to the right was once the site of a shrine known as Mizu (water) Inari. In this case we know what the name commemorates. During the Edo period the water that bubbled out of the spring was known for its curative powers. In 1820 a massive stone torii was erected to mark the spot. The spring disappeared long ago and the torii has been moved to the new location of the shrine, our next destination.

Walk back up the hill and turn right at a corner with five intersecting streets. Here is another back-street-delightful experience with shops for everyday necessities and a few of special interest (one a neighborhood buy-sell shop; stop in, you may find a bargain).

Along the way you may see the tired remains of what was once a majestic old shiinoki (sweet acorn) tree which in other days was encircled by a Shinto rope to commemorate its venerable age, said to be more than 500 years. Until recently it had a companion, Tokyo's oldest enju tree. The English translation of that name may lead to pleasant contemplation: Chinese scholar's tree. It is held in high esteem in both China and Japan: every part of it can be used. In the summer it pleases the eye with its yellow, butterfly-like blossoms, which, along with the young leaves, can be boiled and eaten or used to make tea; the buds are used for dyeing and medicines, and after you have eaten the fruit from the pod, the pod can be used to make a soaplike product. The highly prized wood is used in furniture making and in decorating Japanese-style rooms.

Years ago there was a five-story pagoda here. It was destroyed during the wartime bombings; only the trees remain. The property is presently a parking lot, but once it belonged to a daimyo family. A part of the estate is preserved at Kansen-en (甘泉園), a garden that you will reach after passing a newer type of Tokyo estate—apartment houses.

Walk along the wide path that edges the park. It leads to the new Mizu Inari (水稲荷) shrine, its stone torii the one that was moved here from the former location near Ana Hachiman.

This area was once a riding ground (remember the name of the station?) and now, in October, those days are recalled as riders reenact one of the skills of the samurai, yabusame, a combination of precision archery and horsemanship with riders dressed in old armor (or modern copies) galloping down the path and speeding arrows toward targets located alongside without changing pace or even looking where they are aiming, and usually splitting the wooden target right down the middle.

Return along the path to the garden entrance and wind your way to the bottom of the hill, passing by a little stream and a pretty pond. Here was where the daimyo's mansion once stood. Do look back when you reach the road below. The curve of the roof of Mizu Inari, glimpsed through the trees, is one of those rare, only-in-the-Orient views almost too typical to be real.

At the bottom of the hill you'll once again find the streetcar tracks that wander in and out of our story. Tokyo was once criss-crossed with streetcar lines. Now only two remain, and they both may be gone by the time you read this–but not if sentimental citizens have their way. For a bit of nostalgia, you might want to take a ride, perhaps back to Otsuka Station. It will only cost ¥120, but that, too, is subject to change.

There may be some who remember streetcar parties, introduced in Occupation days. It was possible to rent a streetcar and ride through Tokyo with a car full of friends. The streetcar would be decorated in floral splendor and a bar would be set up at one end. It was a joyful, and often hilarious, party that was transported through the city streets.

You can still rent a streetcar but the good old party days are over. What you get now is a trip from one end of the line to the other. No bar, no decorations (unless you do them yourself), but the cost is still reasonable.

In recent years, a rakugoka (teller of traditional stories) has occasionally chartered one to weave tales of old Edo for his admirers as his "stage" weaves its way through the streets of modern Tokyo.

Streetcars are still known by their old name, chin-chin-densha, a combination that sounds like the starting bell that rings out at each corner. It should be noted that this streetcar line, linking Waseda University to Minowabashi, makes the trip in forty minutes even during rush hours when cars and buses may need well over an hour for the same distance. Streetcars, you may remember, were sacrificed to make way for more modern methods of transportation.

Cross the tracks and you will see the Kanda River, once lined with cherry trees, a popular picnic site. The name of the bridge to the left dates back to Heian days. The story: a court nobleman, crossing the bridge, saw the face of his beloved, then in Kyoto, traced in the shadows. The bridge was consequently given a romantic and sentimental name—Omokage-bashi (Reflection Bridge). The original arched wooden bridge has long since disappeared (you can still see it in woodblock prints), but the name has been preserved, a romantic tribute to a distant love.

Hold tight to that lovely old scene as you return to the station along narrow streets that still wander but would seldom inspire thoughts of romance.

Perhaps you have noticed a peculiar revolving statue from the station. Water from an umbrella-shaped fountain continuously flows over the gold-colored plastic figures causing them to glow like the metal they symbolize. One is obviously a sumo wrestler, but the other? It is Marilyn Monroe, a striking combination created by a popular illustrator of comic books to attract attention to the enterprise whose offices it marks. No one will have trouble finding his/her way to the doors of Suzuya,[1] Japan's (and probably the world's) most successful pawnshop with a turnover of more than $4.5 billion a year.

Yoshi Suzuki, with two small children to support after the war, decided to open a pawnshop. Her first customer was a student who wanted a loan of ¥2,000 on his tattered uniform. It was well above its value but she gave it to him because it was her first transaction. He thanked her profusely. He hadn't eaten in three days, he said, and with ¥2,000, he could eat for twenty. She continues to accept almost anything and interest rates are well below average.

Now in her 80s, she says her only recreation is mahjong, which she plays 25 days out of each month. Her one regret is that she has never sailed around the world on the Queen Elizabeth.

1. Suzuya, 4-6-6 Takadanobaba, Shinjuku-ku; tel. 362-0101
　　スズヤ　新宿区高田馬場 4-6-6

THE DANCHI LIFE STYLE

Shin Okubo: New Big Hollow

SHIN OKUBO IS A SUBURB within the center of the city. Once it was considered a part of the outskirts of Shinjuku, then in the distant reaches of Edo. Now Shinjuku has become one of the several hearts of Tokyo, and Shin Okubo has long since lost its suburban characteristics.

In today's Japan, suburbs are more often known as "bed towns." This is an appropriate name for the area around Shin Okubo Station. The land, once owned by the Japanese army, has been given over to a vast housing area. More than five thousand families call these city-owned, high-rise "apatos" home. In addition, there are

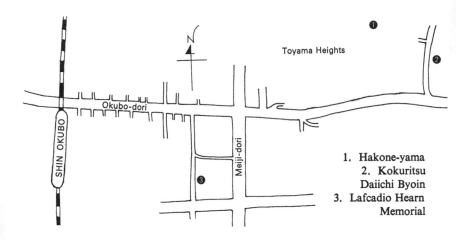

1. Hakone-yama
2. Kokuritsu
   Daiichi Byoin
3. Lafcadio Hearn
   Memorial

numerous other government and private housing complexes in the area.

Turn to the right after leaving the station and walk about eight hundred meters. You will see many tall buildings after you cross Meiji-dori. These are danchi, a new word coined to cover a new life style—nuclear families living in apartment cities. Danchi have been responsible for a change in the standard dimensions of Japan, which once were based on the size of a tatami mat. Since the decision was made to make mats slightly smaller for the danchi, a whole new range of danchi-sized furniture has been manufactured. It fits better in the small apartments, but with the Japanese growing larger with each generation, it hardly fits the people it is designed for.

Another new addition to the nation's vocabulary is the abbreviation 3DK. This is the most common size for the newer danchi apartments, three rooms (not counting bathing and toilet facilities) and a kitchen with space for dining. To Westerners, it is incredible that families can live in such small quarters, the apartment size for a family of four generally falling somewhere between 160 and 220 square feet. To the Japanese, accustomed to efficient space utilization (the living room is quickly transformed into a bedroom at night) and resigned, because of prohibitively high land costs, never to own their own homes, the 3DK has become, if not the realization of an ideal, at least a haven. The relatively low cost is some compensation in these days of inflation. Rents on the city-owned apartments in this area range from around ¥20,000 to ¥30,000, and the government picks up a generous percentage of that amount.

It should be noted that these apartments are for low-income families. Demand is so much greater than availability that residents are chosen by lottery. Those who don't qualify for government housing must go the agent route with its added-on fees and deposits. What they get is an apartment in a building called a mansion in Japan, even though the size is generally even smaller than the government apartments. The price? Unbelievable.

Visualize what it would be like to live here. Think of Shin Okubo Station in the mornings as the mainly white-collar workers head for their offices, and of the wives who must fulfill their lives within the tiny dimensions of their danchi apartments.

You can, if you like, take the elevator to the top of one of the larger apartments for a view of the city spread out below. You may feel that you are in a cage—strong bars enclose the roof to prevent careless falls or planned suicides. The maze of buildings below is broken occasionally by the curve of a temple roof, a patch of trees that marks a shrine or a garden.

The rather desolate area to the north has been cleared for future construction projects that will result in more look alike danchi. Here you will find a small hill with a circling path leading to the top. How could you guess that what you see is all that remains of a carefully constructed reproduction of the Hakone mountain area, a favorite resort for Tokyo (and Edo) residents? This was once a a wondrous park, created by the Owari branch of the Tokugawa family to represent in miniature the fifty-three stages of the Tokaido. (The Mito branch busied itself with Korakuen, one of Tokyo's most famous gardens. It's near Korakuen Station on the Marunouchi

Subway Line.) You won't find anything today to remind you of the real Hakone mountains here among the tall buildings, yet there is more than a memory. What remains of the mountain is 44.6 meters above sea level. It is the highest land in the city.

The Tokyo municipal government once had different plans for this area. In 1948 it was decided to preserve it as a zoological garden. Instead, Occupation authorities decided that this should be the setting for a modern housing development. The thousand units that were built here were known as Toyama Heights and became the model for group housing throughout Japan. These independent houses have been torn down to be replaced by the more-people-per-tatami danchi. There was once a monument at the top of the imitation Hakone-yama to the American colonel who made the decision to construct a housing area instead of a park. I suppose a lot of people would like to thank him for his dream of independent houses in the suburbs, yet wouldn't it be nice to have a miniature Hakone mountain right in the middle of Tokyo?

You can easily climb to the top of this Hakone mountain. The tall building beyond it is Kokuritsu Daiichi Byoin, a national hospital. The monument you'll pass on the circling path records the history of Hakone-yama. Looking north from the mini-mountain top, you'll see a bluff topped with large buildings. This is the all-girls branch of Gakushuin, the school that was once open only to the titled aristocracy. Classes are held here for junior and senior high school, and for a two-year college course that prepares the students for careers and/or marriage. For other ages, Gakushuin is coeducational. Someone, sometime, decided that there should be separation during this impressionable time of life.

Now you can return to the station, pondering on all you've seen, and wondering how you could adapt to danchi living. Think too of the titled aristocracy with the leisure, the inclination, the ability, and the money to create a scale model of the Tokaido. Stop at the stores in the danchi buildings and decide what you'd buy if you were planning dinner, or wonder what it would be like to return to one of these apartments after work. Likely you too would stop on the way to enjoy a beer or a bottle of sakè with friends. Perhaps it would be for the pleasure of companionship, or perhaps it would be to delay a little longer the return to your 3DK.

Lafcadio Hearn, at the turn of the century, wrote with great love and sensitivity of another Japan. He must have drawn inspiration for some of his stories from the area you are walking through for he lived for a while in a small house just off the main street. It's located near Okubo Shogakko (primary school) at 2–265 Nishi Okubo (西大久保 2 の 265). There is a wall surrounding the house, and, imbedded in the wall, an old stone monument that marks it as Hearn's house. We can only wonder what Hearn would write if he could see what's happened to his old home town.

WHICH WAY?

Shinjuku: New Post Town

SHINJUKU IS two stories—east side, west side. The east-side story is one of shopping by day and amusements by night. The west-side story is of commerce, with a new city center pushing skyward in a cluster of Japan's tallest buildings.

As a center for entertainment, Shinjuku east has managed to be a great deal to a large number of people, mainly those whose suburban housing lies alongside the commuter lines that terminate at Shinjuku Station. Here rush hours are not limited to the morning and evening crush. There is also the great midnight exodus when tipsy white-collar playboys head home on the last train to their waiting wives.

Some eighty years ago Shinjuku was a fork in the road surrounded by paddy fields. It wasn't until travelers reached Yotsuya that credentials were checked at a wooden gate, the entrance to Edo.

In the late 17th century, lodgings for travelers were built at Shinjuku (the name can also be translated as "new lodgings"). It rapidly gained the reputation it has kept through the years as an amusement center with emphasis more on variety than quality. The amusements became so questionable that in 1720 the area was closed down for some fifty years, and a great number of the so-called waitresses of Shinjuku were forced to find employment in the legally licensed quarters where there was no need to masquerade their profession. Shinjuku reverted to a village state which continued until after the Meiji Restoration.

When it was announced in the 1880s that a train station would be built in Shinjuku, the residents complained. They said it would be bad for the crops. But progress could not be stopped, even though it is recorded that on rainy days "there wasn't a soul to be seen anywhere about." This is quite in contrast to the opening of the present Shinjuku Station Building in May, 1964. The first day, 1,700,000 passengers were counted. Since then, the number has grown to more than two million on an average day.

The farmers' fears were well founded. The coming of the train brought new life to the country town, and when other lines terminated at the station, its growth was assured. Still, it wasn't until the great Kanto quake of 1923 that Shinjuku really emerged. Fate had chosen to spare, for the most part, this outer edge of the city, and Shinjuku had its first taste of being a center. Local stores flourished since people had few other places to shop, and Tokyo's growth momentum was directed westward into the Musashino plains with Shinjuku as the hub.

1. Kanto Electric
2. Takano Fruit Parlor
3. Isetan Department Store
4. Keio Plaza Hotel
5. Sumitomo Building
6. KDD Communications Center
7. Mitsui Building
8. Shinjuku Imperial Gardens

World War II was not so kind, but the area was quickly rebuilt along with the rest of the city, all the while expanding its special characteristic: that of a sakariba (amusement center).

The amusements are many. Noting the number of pictures and posters promising the sensual delights to be found at the backstreet bars and clubs, it comes as no surprise that in postwar times the first Western-style striptease/burlesque theater was located in Shinjuku. However, it was only the Western influence that was new. In spite of the often-repeated claim (or blame), the striptease was not a gift from the Occupation forces.

Japan's own striptease dates back to the days when Amaterasu-omikami, the sun goddess, was tempted out of the cave where she was hiding (thus thrusting the world into darkness) by a spirited dancer who prompted enough audience response by removing her clothes to cause the deity to leave her seclusion to see what the fun was all about. Any who have seen the deft handling of a fan by a traditional strip artist will feel that in this form of amusement there wasn't a great deal that the West could teach the East. Another old-time favorite is the woman warrior whose multi-layer kimono are snippy-snapped off one by one by the deftly wielded swords of a band of samurai. You'll find them all, along with porno films and burlesque theaters, along the backstreets of Shinjuku.

You'll also find the area's bow to culture preserved in a name. The famous old Kabuki Theater, in the East Ginza district, had been gutted by incendiary bombing in the last year of World War II, and there were plans to rebuild it in Shinjuku. In the end, however, a new Kabuki Theater was built within the remaining walls of the old, and all that's left of the Shinjuku dream is a section called Kabuki-cho and a cluster of movie theaters. Don't miss it—and don't wait too long to find it. Much of this picturesque area is soon to disappear, another sacrifice to beautification and street widening. Best is the short street lined with seafood restaurants that effectively tempt customers with salesman-cooks in front who broil delicacies over charcoal grills. Stop for one of the giant shrimp and you'll probably stay for the evening.

In the '60s, the Shinjuku image—late-night bars and coffee shops, questionable go-go parlors and teahouses, cheap shops and run-down lodgings, with easy access from everywhere—drew the newly emerged futen and their foreign counterparts, the hippies. They found a home in Shinjuku, sleeping in 150-yen-a-night rooms when not camped out at the east exit of the station. The station plaza also became the center for the activities of Beheiren, the Japan Peace for Vietnam Committee. On Saturday nights they held sing-ins where bearded, long-haired Japanese strummed guitars and sang popular American protest songs that had little meaning to most Japanese. Almost as big a crowd of policemen would be on hand to keep things under control.

It says something for the Japanese view of delinquent youth that when the police finally moved in earnest to clean up the area, the campaign was known as Operation Sunflower. It was a successful maneuver, with the owners of many of the favorite hangouts seeking police guidance in creating a new image. A few places hung on for a while, including the popular Fugetsudo, a coffee and music shop which finally closed a few years ago, but many remember to listen ing to Donovan and the Rolling Stones in the dark and crowded room. It was a short but exciting period for a suddenly apparent young sub-culture, a small irritation on the surface of the smoothly operating system.*

People have always been cleaning up Shinjuku, but there's a lot left that could stand a little polishing. For those who want to explore the seamier side, look for those sidestreet, run-down areas filled with tiny bars and neon signs. Be wary of places with unposted prices. They usually have someone around to see that you pay their excessively high bills. But you'll be safe enough among the other curious strollers. Do be sensible, though, giving due con-

---

* Now Japan's "children" dance on Sundays near Harajuku Station

sideration to the language barrier and the differences in customs.

A bit about the area behind Kanto Electric on the map. It is true that prostitution is illegal in Japan. It is equally true that the narrow bar-lined streets with girls (and farther along, boys) sitting in doorways give an impression of what the rooms above the bars might possibly be used for. Don't jump to that conclusion, however. Today's more affluent pleasure seekers prefer love hotels, and there are plenty of them around. Now the rooms are most often living quarters for the gang-oriented men who manage the street activities and who are always close at hand in case any trouble develops. Perhaps that's why a friendly police box was built into the corner of the electric company building. Yet the streets beyond seem unchanged, rather like a movie set for scenes of solicitation.

There's also a wholesome side to Shinjuku's east side. See it in the bright plastic splendor on the sixth floor of the Takano Fruit Parlor (高野フルツパーラー), a food palace with special sections devoting their efforts to typical foods from India, Germany, the U.S., Italy . . . an international roundup at reasonable prices that gives the taste of travel to the mostly young crowd that fills the tables. The ground on which Takano sits is worth around ¥8 million a square meter. Think about that as you eat your cheap lunch.

The east side also offers shopping, at boutiques and specialty shops as well as at large department stores. Isetan is especially popular with foreigners.

Head west to see what else is going on in Shinjuku, a new complex of tall buildings constructed over the old Yodobashi water-purification reservoir. First was the forty-seven-story Keio Plaza Hotel, followed shortly after by Sumitomo's hollow-centered headquarters and the KDD communications center. Now, with eleven buildings, that project is completed. But the construction isn't over, and new skyscrapers like the new NS building and the computerized Washington Hotel are scheduled to become Shinjuku landmarks. The plan is to limit buildings to 66 stories or 250 meters, the size that was selected because it would "maintain the beauty of the area." That height is also claimed to be safe in a major earthquake. Once, in Tokyo, there were many views of Mount Fuji. Next it was Tokyo Tower we could see from almost anywhere. Now it is Shinjuku's skyscrapers.

Sometime you should take the time to explore this mini-Manhattan. Take the Sumitomo Building, for example, its first-floor focus of interest a huge prism that reflects the sky and refracts the upper stories which line their hallways with a fantastic array of day and night restaurants that serve a gourmet's assortment of specialties. There's a culture center sponsored by the Asahi newspaper which provides an astonishing number of classes—230—in such subjects as Man'yoshu poetry, politics, kung-fu, and kimono wearing. There's an extensive arched arcade on the ground floor with restaurants and shops, and across the way, the Do Sports Plaza, which includes everything you'd normally think of plus facilities for deep-sea diving and water-skiing practice. The Mitsui tower has one of the world's largest high-in-the-sky Chinese restaurants, and the Keio Plaza Hotel provides a top-floor bar where you can watch the trains go by way down below as you enjoy your favorite concoction.

While a lot has been going up, there's quite a bit going down as well. The station's underground shopping area claims 120 stores and a huge underground parking lot. It boasts an anti-disaster computer system that should allow down-under shoppers to feel secure. Even so, the government is now concerned about the safety of such complexes in case of an earthquake or fire and this may be among the last to receive official approval.

Finally, there's one more Shinijuku pleasure—Shinjuku Imperial Gardens (Shinjuku Gyoen, 新宿御苑). Actually, it is way over in East Shinjuku, lying about midway between Shinjuku Station and our next stop, Yoyogi Station, which means that we're treating it out of geographical logic. But, certainly for garden lovers, it's worth a special visit of its own. Even from Shinjuku Station it's quite a walk, and you might prefer to save on shoe leather by transferring from the Yamanote Line at Shinjuku Station to the Marunouchi Subway Line and riding two stops to the subway station called Shinjuku Gyoenmae, which lets you out practically at the entrance to the gardens.

These gardens were once the estate of a daimyo family by the name of Naito. In fact, when the distance from Nihon-bashi to Shimotakaido on the Koshu-kaido proved to be much too long for easy travel and a new post town was established between these two points, it was originally called Naito Shinjuku (Naito's New Post Town). In the years since then the name has been shortened to simply Shinjuku, but the old name also lingers on in the Japanese love of playing with words: now it's often called Night Shinjuku, the English word being pronounced the same as Naito. And anyone who visits Shinjuku after dark will soon discover how apt the name is.

But back to the garden itself. After the Meiji Restoration the area became an imperial preserve and then, after World War II, a public park. It is famous for its great variety of cherry trees and serves as a lovely site for the cherry-viewing party that the prime minister gives yearly for Japanese and foreign dignitaries. Even more spectacular than the cherry blossoms are the chrysanthemums in November. You just can't know how many kinds of chrysanthemums can be trained to spectacular perfection until you view the many varieties on display in small woodsy booths along the wandering paths in Shinjuku Gyoen.

代々木

THE DILIGENT STUDENT

Yoyogi: Tree of Many Generations

IT WASN'T MANY YEARS AGO that the Yamanote Line marked the outer boundary of Tokyo. Anything beyond was rice fields, woods, and farmhouses. Less than a half-century ago, writers referred to the area near the station as Yoyogi Forest. And in that forest there was evidently one venerable old tree that gave the area its name.

The idea of a forest in Yoyogi may seem highly unlikely as you stand in front of the station today wondering which of the angling congested streets to follow. Why not try the wide one on the left? It leads to Meiji Shrine, where you will find a forest after all. By itineraries, the shrine belongs to Harajuku Station, next on our route, but there is much to see there and little to see here. Our suggestion: walk to Harajuku through what remains of Yoyogi Forest savoring your stroll along the wide, quiet pathways of Meiji Shrine.

If your interest is cameras, look for the D.P.E. photo shop of Kamio Ishii[1] as you walk toward Meiji Shrine. He has packed a remarkable collection of old cameras into a tiny window showcase with more spilling out onto the shelves of his small shop. You are welcome to look around. Like any enthusiast, he is happy to talk about his hobby—in Japanese.

Let's choose another street, the one to the left that crosses the tracks. It will lead you to a building that may remind you, not surprisingly, of a printing office. It is the headquarters of the Japan Communist Party (日本共産党本部). If you read Japanese, stop in for a pamphlet or two or the current issue of the official newspaper *Akahata* (Red Flag).

You may have found yourself in the midst of hundreds of students when you got off the train. They are heading down a different street. All are enrolled at a typically Japanese institution, Yoyogi Seminar,[2] a school with only one purpose: to prepare students for the entrance exams that must be passed before they can be admitted to any of the prestigious universities. And without the proper degree from the right university, it is a rare person who will find a successful place in the firmly established web of Japanese society.

There are many such schools in Japan but this is the largest and the most famous. Students come from all over the country to attend, with the number of enrollees running as high as 120,000 during the special summer sessions. Students, acutely aware of learning levels

1. Ishii Camera-ten, 1–18–1 Yoyogi, Shibuya-ku; tel. 370–3873
石井カメラ店 渋谷区代々木 1–18–1
2. Yoyogi Seminar, 1–27–16 Yoyogi, Shibuya-ku; tel. 379–5221
代々木ゼミナール 渋谷区代々木 1–27–16

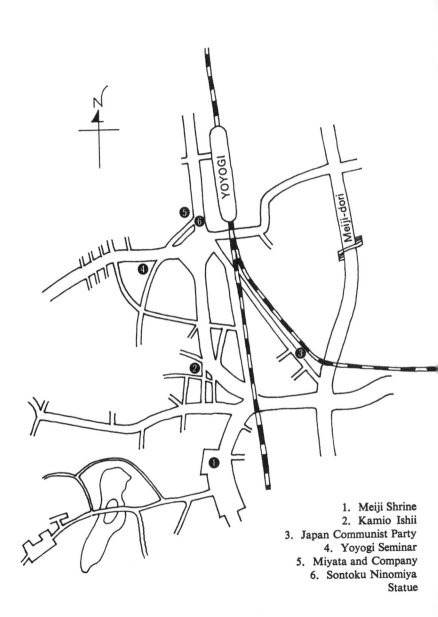

YOYOGI

Meiji-dori

1. Meiji Shrine
2. Kamio Ishii
3. Japan Communist Party
4. Yoyogi Seminar
5. Miyata and Company
6. Sontoku Ninomiya Statue

and school requirements, can judge accurately which school they stand a good chance of being admitted to by comparing their accomplishments with those of their classmates.

The system leads to many of the phenomena of Japanese society. For one, there is the "education mama" who pushes her child constantly to the highest possible achievement. Family life revolves around the student's needs. The mother's efforts are dedicated to his success, and there are few sacrifices she will not make to assure it. In the meantime, the child follows a routine of study (but only of those subjects that will prepare him properly for the next step up the ladder) with little time for carefree relaxation. In the end, the successful education mama can meet her old school friends with her head held high; her son has passed through all the proper schools from kindergarten up and now has a position with Hitachi or Mitsui or the Foreign Office and is assured lifetime security. And so is she, for he will be able to take care of her in her old age, which likely will start with her son's marriage to a girl proper for his position.

The system also helps maintain the male-oriented society. Yes, girls are now competing for entrance to good universities and are being more widely employed, but most of them will make their own proper marriage before the age of twenty-five and continue the cycle. The men start their circle of close acquaintances early in life, and their best friends are also the ones with whom they are locked in the deepest competition. So they study together, play together, and later work together, constantly trying to assure their own security within the group. They can't ignore the group or they won't know what's going on. From the youngest age, being a part of the group becomes essential; there's no proper place for a loner.

Many of today's young people are trying to break out of these stereotypes, but old goals and methods to achieve them are hard to change. And we mustn't overlook the fact that the system works. Companies quote statistics showing that graduates of top-ranked universities contribute more (effort/loyalty/expertise) than other employees. On a broader scale, look what Japan has accomplished over the last thirty years.

So mingle awhile with the students, browse in their bookstores, have a cheap bowl of soba at any of the numerous, student-filled restaurants. You'll find a number of pamphlets in the open lobby of the main building. Look at the pictures of all the fun you can have, the camaraderie you can enjoy, the friends you'll make, the memories you'll store, if you dedicate yourself to preparing for those entrance examinations at Yoyogi Seminar. Because once you see your name on the acceptance list of your chosen university, you have it made for life.

There's one more thing. The students provide an all-covering excuse for the local businessmen. They can't get on those crowded trains after work and have to stop off at a local bar for a beer or two until the student rush hour is over before returning home.

Let's try another street, this time to the right. Your destination, Miyata and Company,[3] famous for silversmithing. On the way you'll pass a small memorial beside a sushi shop. There is a statue of a boy carrying a load on his back and a book in his hand, obviously trudging along under adverse conditions. While it suggests the local daytime student population, it actually commemorates the shop owner's frequent visits to a nearby shrine. The statue is a famous one and you'll see it often in Japan. I thought for years it was a book-laden student on his way to school. Instead, it is Sontoku Ninomiya carrying wood for cooking. He was a poor man's son who had to work every day but still managed to find time to study and achieve success through diligence and determination. This is exactly the kind of model Japanese students have always needed. O.K. Time for the next class.

There are many who remember Miyata when it was housed in a rambling, Japanese-style house that stood where the present build-

3. Miyata and Co., 1–38–2 Yoyogi, Shibuya-ku; tel. 379–4726
　宮田宝石店　渋谷区代々木 1–38–2

ing now is. Silver has always been Miyata's business and in a day when craftsmen worked for pleasure instead of money and precious metals were cheap, people brought their old silver pieces here to have them copied with workmanship often superior to the original and prices considerably less. But that was a long time ago. Miyata is still recognized as Tokyo's leading silversmith and will make things to order if you can't find what you want on the well-filled shelves.

There are other streets to explore alongside the station; follow them if you like. We would like to refer you to the second paragraph, however. There's nothing like a walk in a forest, especially if you are in the center of Tokyo.

POETRY IN STEEL AND CONCRETE

Harajuku: Post Town in the Fields

THERE HAS BEEN something inevitable about the development of
Harajuku. A large part of this area was once the Yoyogi Rempeijo,
extensive parade and training grounds for the Japanese army. Of
course there were also many cherry trees; the two go together in
Japan—the symbolism of the beauty of cherry blossoms, fading so
soon, and youth which passes so quickly.

Then it was inevitable that after Emperor Meiji's death, in 1912,
a shrine would be built to his memory. This beautiful area was the
obvious site, somewhat secluded as it was from the busy city
growing up around it.

And it was inevitable that the Occupation forces should take over the space formerly used by the Japanese military. It became Washington Heights, a bit of displaced America in the heart of Tokyo with roomy duplexes and grassy lawns. The mini-city contained all that anyone needed—movie theaters, churches, supermarkets, PXs. People never really had to go outside the gates. But how much they missed if they didn't!

Now the military image is no longer evident in Japan and the area has a different face. In 1964 the world was invited to come and look at the new Japan as the nation hosted the first Olympic Games ever to be held in Asia. Of course a large expanse of conveniently located land was necessary—and there was Washington Heights, no longer a requirement of the U.S. military with the Occupation at an end. Washington Heights became a housing area for the visiting athletes and the site of two of Tokyo's most impressive buildings. Designed by Kenzo Tange, they are a dedication to sports which captures in concrete and steel the simplicity of a Shinto shrine, the massive strength suggested by a Buddhist temple—and for those less esoteric, they symbolize the butterfly swimmer's stroke, the baseketball player's leap. The images remain though the buildings now show their age.

Of course the Olympic grounds necessitated an extensive information center and, with the Olympics over, what better place to relocate the crowded facilities of NIIK, Nippon Hoso Kyokai, Japan's public TV-radio network, with space left over for an expansive public park.

Finally, the Harajuku area, internationalized by the Occupation and the Olympics, has become one of the most cosmopolitan sections of the city, its emphasis still on youth. Today's young people, consumer-oriented, are far removed from the warriors of yesterday, who found fulfillment in dying for their country; they're also quite different from the disciplined athletes of the 1964 Olympics. But the cherry blossoms still fall, their message as inevitable as the passing of the seasons.

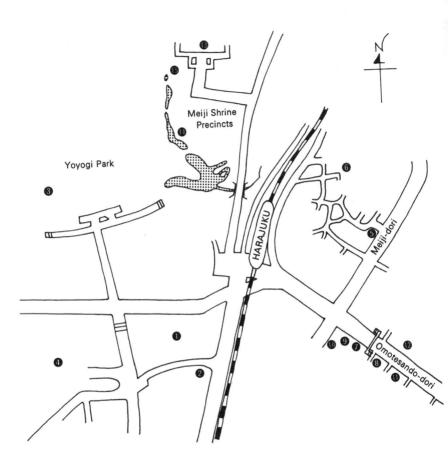

1. Olympic buildings
2. Kishi Memorial Hall
3. Yoshitoshi Tokugawa Memorial
4. NHK
5. Togo Shrine
6. Seicho no Ie
7. Fuji Torii
8. Oriental Bazaar
9. Kiddy Land
10. Shimura
11. Tokyo Union Church
12. Dojunkai Apartments
13. Meiji Shrine
14. Iris Garden
15. Kiyomasa no Ido

With all this, where to start? Let's make it a view of Tange's inspiring Olympic buildings seen from the top of the overpass just beyond the station. The smaller structure, resembling a graceful seashell, was for basketball and other indoor games, the larger, with its magnificent sweeping roof, for swimming. You can go inside if you like, viewing swimming or ice skating, depending on the season. The area is known as the Yoyogi Sports Center and includes many sports-related facilities. Such a large, open space is rare in Tokyo, and many come simply to enjoy the view of the expansive, grass-covered slopes. This is one of the few places where you will see people walking on the grass.

There are memories too. Look for the bronze bust of Yoshitoshi Tokugawa, Japan's first aviator, who earned his place in history by being airborne for four minutes and traveling seventy meters on December 19, 1910. You can see his plane at the Transportation Museum, described in the Kanda chapter.

Leaving sports behind, you'll reach the completely computerized headquarters of NHK,[1] an engineering achievement that is probably unmatched anywhere in the world. Fortunately, you can learn all about it from a well-organized tour. You may find yourself in a perfect reproduction of an Edo mansion where any samurai would feel at home, or watching the satellite-transmitted review of today's news from anywhere. Just push a button.

If it is Sunday, on the wide street between the station and NHK, you will see the young of Tokyo dancing to each group's chosen beat and dressed to match the music (there the Elvis Presleys, there the James Deans, "bamboo children" over there), an enthusiastic outpouring of group-oriented individuality.

Now stroll along Meiji-dori crowded with Japan's first-ever wealthy, luxury-oriented younger generation enjoying what their parents never had: leisure.

---

1. NHK, 2-2-1 Jinnan, Shibuya-ku; tel. 465-1111
　日本放送協会　渋谷区神南 2-2-1

In the midst of all this heady activity, there is Togo Jinja,[2] a venerable shrine dedicated to one of Japan's greatest heroes, Tsushima Straits led to the disastrous defeat of the Russian navy in 1905 in the Russo-Japanese War, an unexpected event that caused the rest of the world to become suddenly aware that Japan had joined the other "civilized" nations. The shrine has a cooperative arrangement with the Admiral Nimitz Center in Fredricksburg, Texas, for a sharing of exhibits. The American naval hero was a great admirer of Japan's Admiral Togo and contributed personally to the restoration of his flagship, the Mikasa, now in Yokosuka, and to Togo Shrine. Classes in pottery making (many foreigners attend) are held in the Togo Yochien (kindergarten) behind the shrine. There is a wedding hall/meeting-room/restaurant building where you can have lunch or dinner, or order a cup of coffee in the attractive lounge that provides a restful view of the attractive Japanese garden.

Another religious group has its headquarters beyond the Togo memorial. This is the Seicho no Ie,[3] founded by Masaharu Taniguchi some fifty years ago. Its goal is a union of all the world's religions. There are reported to be more than three million members. You'll easily identify the building by the tall, spire-topped dome.

Heading away from the station on Omotesando-dori, you will find many more internationalized shops. Among them are some that are favorites of foreigners. When the area was dominated by Washington Heights, it was inevitable that a number of stores would be established outside the gates to supply the peculiar demands of these foreigners. A few are still there, with some of the best bargains in town (military people have always been good shoppers). Over the years, store owners learned what foreigners

2. Togo Shrine, 1-5-3 Jingumae, Shibuya-ku; tel. 403-3591
   東郷神社　渋谷区神宮前 1-5-3
3. Seicho no Ie, 1–23–30 Jingumae, Shibuya-ku; tel. 401–0131
   生長の家　渋谷区神宮前 1-23-30

prefer, and they still supply them at prices that often can't be matched elsewhere. A shopping excursion along Omotesando can provide almost anything you'll want at such stores as Fuji Torii and Oriental Bazaar for antiques, art goods, and souvenirs, and Kiddy Land for toys and novelties.

Further along the street is the Tokyo Union Church,[4] established more than a hundred years ago to provide a place of worship for Tokyo's Christians, then mostly missionaries, of any sect or nationality. Across the street are the Dojunkai Apartments, which were built after the Great Earthquake of 1923 with donations received from within Japan and from all over the world. They were completed in 1926, splendid, all-concrete structures that were much admired by visitors. Now the shabby, run-down buildings seem out of place, a rather embarrassing poor relation at today's feast of plenty.

Saturday afternoon and Sunday are especially good days for Harajuku youth-culture viewing. At one time, in the mid '60s, it was the congregation center for a youth suddenly turned on by the new prosperity, children with parents wealthy enough to permit luxuries undreamed of by prewar families. First notice came from neighboring residents who complained to the police about the loud noise from the late-at-night motorists gunning their cars and motorcycles as they raced along the wide boulevards. The police, always tolerant, took a typical Japanese countermeasure. Each evening they would gather together thirty or forty of these "wild youths" and give them "guidance talks." This strategy had no effect whatsoever.

Today, with young people more accustomed to luxuries, the emphasis has shifted to shopping and eating. Well dressed and well fed, Japan's new wave of young people walk along the wide sidewalks holding hands (another postwar development) and enjoying their role in today's consumer-oriented society. Also rep-

4. Tokyo Union Church, 5–7–7 Jingumae, Shibuya-ku; tel. 400–0047
東京ユニオン教会　渋谷区神宮前 5-7-7

resented are members of the sub-culture, long-haired and jean-clad, selling handcrafted goods on mats laid out along the sidewalks.

Now back to the station and Meiji Shrine, one of the most revered in all Japan. It is dedicated to Emperor Meiji, who led the nation out of its feudal isolation and into the world community of nations. The Meiji Restoration of 1868 took the power from the weakened shogunate and restored it to the emperor, a direct descendant, it is claimed, of Emperor Jimmu, the first ruler of Japan, whose reign was so long ago that history is easily blended with myth. Following the Meiji Restoration, Edo became Tokyo, the daimyo disbanded their samurai, and one of the most unusual periods in the annals of any history came to an end.

Magnificent simplicity could be used to describe this Shinto shrine in an area of huge trees and wandering paths that effectively mask its center-of-the-city location. The huge torii are made of cypress trees from Taiwan which are claimed to have been more than 1,500 years old. There's a treasure house behind the main shrine building which displays various articles used by Emperor Meiji. Among them is the impressive six-horse carriage he used on state occasions.

If you can, visit Meiji Shrine's iris garden in late June or early July. A wandering stream is a proper setting for the spectacular shobu, the wide, flat iris in white and shades of blue, lavender, and purple. You've seen them before, pictured on Japanese screens, decorating fine porcelains, re-created in gold on lustrous black lacquerware. Since ancient times, on Boys' Day (more recently renamed Children's Day) on May 5, the leaves of the shobu are bundled together and used in the bath water. Since they are shaped like swords, they are supposed to impart strength; they are also credited with preventing illness. Once samurai would have a cup of sakè mixed with fragrant, finely chopped iris leaves before going into battle. Then the symbolism was slightly different. *Shobu* as a spoken word also has the meaning of victory.

Beyond the iris garden is Kiyomasa no Ido, a famous old well which has been supplying fresh water for more than four hundred years. It is named for the man who located the water, Kiyomasa Kato, a famous warrior and architect of his day. And in his time, architects were required to design strong castles and to search out good locations for wells to assure an abundant supply of water. You couldn't have one without the other.

There is another "station" at Harajuku (not recognized as a real station by JNR) though few people notice it. You can see it best from the Yoyogi end of the station platform, a Meiji-looking structure on the right. The entrance is at the end of the street that runs alongside the tracks. The platform is for the exclusive use of the Emperor. In this busy area, hardly anyone notices when his entourage arrives, and the Emperor boards his special train. Times are far different from the old days when anyone who lived alongside the tracks was ordered to cover the windows when the Emperor's train passed by. No one was allowed to look upon the "august presence" or the train that carried him. Still, it is said that even now the operator of any train that carries the Emperor must be so skillful that an egg, placed on a plate, will not move as the train accelerates or comes to a stop.

When the Emperor travels on the Shinkansen, he uses the special entrance reserved for the Imperial family and official guests at Tokyo Station. You can see it, at the center of the building, marked by a circular driveway. The marble-lined hallways and reception rooms are not open to the public, but it has been suggested that when the present station building is demolished—as it inevitably will be—to make room for a more practical building, the Emperor's entrance foyer should be incorporated into the new design, a pleasing link between the old and the new.

FAITHFUL HACHIKO

Shibuya: Astringent Valley

IEYASU, THE FIRST TOKUGAWA SHOGUN, passed this way when he first entered Edo. Today, following the same path, he would have found himself in Shibuya, a congestion of traffic, shoppers, perpetual street repairs, demonstrating radicals, second-run theaters, inexpensive restaurants, sidewalk peddlers, Turkish baths, love hotels, and a shopper's paradise of department stores and specialty shops. Had he been faced with all that, Ieyasu might never have found his way on to his new capital.

The plaza in front of the station is a popular meeting place for young people. Radicals also choose it for their demonstrations, a strange sight in democratic Japan. Helmeted men and women, faces hidden by cotton-towel masks, solicit signatures on petitions and harangue the crowd from their loudspeaker trucks. In another country they might be considered forerunners of a revolution and be promptly rounded up and sent off to jail. Here, demonstrations are common and, in typical Japanese fashion, prior approval must be obtained. Even the most radical groups will follow the regulations and march off for the prime minister's residence with the official permit in hand. The police provide an appropriate number of escorts. A frequently repeated story tells how marchers in anti-U.S. demos a number of years ago would break ranks to ask politely for English conversation lessons. Today, most demonstrators are demanding lower rice prices or higher bonuses, but it is wise to stear clear of those with helmets and face masks. Don't be unduly concerned about the loud tirades from uniformed men on high-decible sound trucks, a vocal but (presently) small group of rightists.

But this digression has not been a fair picture of Shibuya. Even when the radicals are there in force, commuters continue to catch their trains and buses, to shop and meet their friends with little notice given to the over-amplified tirade.

Shibuya Station is the terminal for a number of commuter rail and bus lines and the Ginza Line, a subway that, in Shibuya, belies its name with platforms three stories above ground. Shop owners have seen to it that all the commuters' requirements are met. There's everything for everybody.

When young men meet their dates in Shibuya, there's no need to say where. It's always the same place, beside the dog statue in the station plaza. It's an appropriate symbol, a tribute to unswerving devotion. For years, Hachiko met his master there each night. After the master's death in 1925, the loyal pet continued to wait patiently beside the station door until the last train had arrived. The statue was built after his death some ten years later with contributions which came from all over Japan. The present statue was erected in 1948. The original had been melted down for essential metal

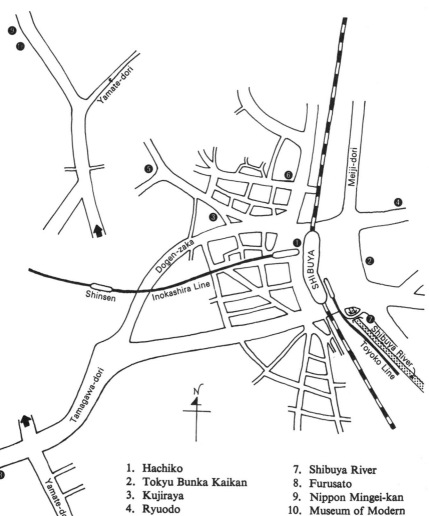

1. Hachiko
2. Tokyu Bunka Kaikan
3. Kujiraya
4. Ryuodo
5. Tokyu Department Store
6. Seibu Department Store
7. Shibuya River
8. Furusato
9. Nippon Mingei-kan
10. Museum of Modern Literature

during World War II. (Incidentally, most feminine names in Japan end with *ko*, meaning "child," which has led to the mistaken impression that Hachiko was female, but he was very much a male dog, the *ko* in his name meaning "daimyo.")

Across from the station's east entrance is the Tokyu Bunka Kaikan, Culture Hall, with a variety of shops, theaters, restaurants, wedding halls, and, on the roof, a planetarium. When the smog first began settling down on Tokyo, there was a sudden increase in the number of planetariums. It was feared that the children would forget what star-filled heavens looked like.

It would seem that Shibuya could feed all of Tokyo in its hundreds of tiny street-level-and-below restaurants. There are also many tall buildings in the station area with restaurants, bars, and nightclubs on each floor, a stunning variety which often leads to complete indecision as one wonders what might be featured upstairs.

Whatever your favorite, there's bound to be a place that specializes in it. For one, there's Kujiraya,[1] a restaurant that serves only whale meat. The Japanese have been subjected to a different set of circumstances regarding whales. Earliest Buddhist dietary taboos prohibited the eating of meat from any four-legged animal. This naturally excluded whales, which have been supplying a major source of inexpensive protein ever since, usually in the form of "sausage" or "ham." The restaurant is always well filled with patrons, although these days you won't find many foreigners among them. The most popular dish is whale served raw, to be dipped in soy sauce before eating.

You'll also find Ryuodo,[2] located under the tracks in front of the station. It deals in snakes, but they are sold for medicine, not food.

1. Kujiraya, 2–29–22 Dogenzaka, Shibuya-ku; tel. 461–9145
   くじら屋　渋谷区道玄坂 2-29-22
2. Ryuodo, 1–13–7 Shibuya, Shibuya-ku; tel. 400–1878
   龍王堂　渋谷区渋谷 1-13-7

Dried, powdered, or soaked in sakè, snake is popular because, they say, it's good for "stamina," the word that suggests sexual prowess in Japan. And men need all they can get. Snakes figure frequently in Japanese legends. They usually assume the form of a woman and always spell disaster for the unfortunate man who, unwittingly, becomes involved with them.

Those interested in more conventional foods of Japan should visit the station building's first floor mini-shops, meiten-gai, branches of some of Japan's most famous food specialty stores. There's a street-fair atmosphere, shouts of "irasshai" (welcome), and crowds of shoppers. It's part of the wandering Toyoko Department Store that wraps itself around the station. The honten (main store) of this well-known enterprise is also in Shibuya but is called by a different name, Tokyu. It's an ideal store for visitors who want an introduction to Japan. There is a free bus service from the station, and for those who drive their own cars, there's ample parking in the basement with polite uniformed attendants who seem to direct foreigners to the most convenient parking slots. Merchandise is all of top quality with specialty sections showing the finest of traditional products. Top-floor restaurants offer a variety of cuisine in attractive and appropriately decorated alcoves. There's usually a bargain-sale section with enough large sizes to make it interesting for foreigners.

There are many eye-catching new buildings such as the gleaming 109 (10–9 is to-kyu in Japanese; it is also the name of the department store that owns it) filled with shops and restaurants. Seibu Department Store also has a Shibuya branch, two stores, one featuring mostly women's things, the other mainly men's.

To the south of the station is one of the most complex of Tokyo's overpasses, crossovers to various corners for shopping or train and bus catching. Once from this vantage point you would have been able to see Shibuya Castle, but that was long ago. Now only the Shibuya name remains.

Below and almost hidden now is the Shibuya River, which supplied the power for the milling industry that flourished here from

Edo days through the 1920s. In early times the milling was done by hand. Later the waterwheel was introduced. In a fashion that would be well understood by today's Japanese industrialists, the milling families met together to allocate their customers so that each mill would be assured of a fair share of the work and the profits. You can see documents pertaining to these agreements at a local museum, the Kyodo Bunkakan, whose exhibits are described in the next chapter. Among them is a Hokusai woodblock print showing a waterwheel beside the Shibuya River. Notice that the water is lifted up from the stream instead of turning the wheel from the top. Of course Mount Fuji can be seen clearly in the background.

Follow the main street behind the station (a splinter street passes a collection of massage parlors known locally as Turkish baths) to the old Yamate-dori, a wide, tree-lined street with many large houses and expensive apartments, exclusive restaurants, and shops for their occupants. Interspaced among them are a number of impressive new embassy buildings, and the Tokyo Baptist Church.

Or continue straight ahead for one of Tokyo's most unusual folk restaurants, Furusato.[3] The menu combines country-inspired specialties with more familiar fare such as huge Hokkaido crab legs that are certain to please anyone. In the summer, guests are invited to indulge in a pleasant country evening pastime (but at city prices). With chopsticks, they fill a bowl with noodles floated on a stream of water circulated by a giant waterwheel in the garden. There's a sauce for dipping. Cold noodles are a favorite throughout Japan. In this setting you can easily understand why. The restaurant also has demonstrations of folk dances. The setting: a three-hundred-year-old farmhouse brought to Tokyo piece by piece from Shirakawa Village. If you ask in advance, you can arrange to have gentle rain dripping from the eaves as you have your dinner.

3. Furusato, 3–4–1 Aobadai, Meguro-ku; tel. 463–2310
　 ふるさと　目黒区青葉台 3-4-1

It has been necessary in this book to place a boundary to our station visits. Consequently, we've left many corners unturned, many streets unexplored. But we'll extend the Shibuya tour to include the Nippon Mingei-kan (Japan Folkcrafts Museum),[4] founded in 1936 by Soetsu Yanagi, the man most responsible for making Japan and the world aware of the country's folk arts, "the natural beauty that springs from the heart and hands of man," as he once described the simple crafts that were being inundated by the advance of mass-produced, look-alike goods. The building, which suggests the simplicity and naturalness of a Japanese farmhouse, is appropriate for the collection. Across the street is the house once used by Yanagi-san. Note the roof. It is made of stone slabs. Its weight is said to be three and a half tons.

Nearby is the old estate of one of Japan's most renowned families, the Maedas; in fact, the museum is located on what was once Maeda property. Postwar changes which eliminated Japan's peerage changed the life style of many of the country's court-related families. A wise path was chosen then by the sixteenth Maeda. He donated much of his property to the government. Other families lost their holdings because of their inability to maintain such huge houses and grounds on a slashed income in a period that granted no privileges to former titleholders. Tokyo University was the recipient of much of the Maeda property.

This decision has made it possible for us to see inside one of the stately European-style mansions once common to the nobility. Today Maeda's mansion is a museum housing literary displays from the Meiji, Taisho, and Showa eras, including books, hand-written manuscripts, and photographs.[5] Even though you may not be able to read the books or the descriptions, you will enjoy wandering among the well-displayed exhibits, picturing the grandeur of the

4. Japan Folkcrafts Museum, 4-3-33 Komaba, Meguro-ku; tel. 467-4527
   日本民芸館　目黒区駒場 4-3-33
5. Tokyo Museum of Modern Literature, 4-3-55 Komaba, Meguro-ku;
   東京都近代文学博物館　目黒区駒場 4-3-55　　　　　　　tel. 466-5150

setting in a day when Japan's nobility modeled its activities on a composite of Europe's finest.

It is not only Europeans who can appreciate its merits. This was the residence selected by General Matthew Ridgway for his use during the Occupation.

There are still Japanese women who remember the general because of his wife's hats. She had so many, they say, and it seemed she always wore a different one. Japanese women had never before seen such elaborate combinations of ribbons, veils, and flowers, and they often waited in front of the mansion for hours to catch a glimpse of her, caring little for her famous husband, the general.

SUMO MEMORIES

Ebisu: Blessings and Long Life

EBISU IS ONE of the seven gods of good luck, usually shown with a
fishing rod in one hand and a large fish in the other. But this part of
Tokyo got its name not directly from the god, but from a beer. In
fact, two of Japan's popular beverages claim this area as home.
Ebisu Station was first opened as a freight depot to transport Ebisu
beer and other products from the industrial belt that lined the Shibuya and Meguro rivers. Today the brewery makes both Ebisu and
Sapporo beer. It covers a wooded hill in what is mainly a residential
area. Except for occasional glimpses of factory-like buildings and
stacks of bright red beer cases, you might think that the old stone

wall enclosed a large estate. If you want to visit the plant, phone in advance to make arrangements.[1]

Near the brewery is a bridge crossing the railroad tracks. For many years it was known as American Bridge in recognition of the American engineer who was in charge of the construction project. Across the bridge and down the hill is the head office and former factory site of Calpis, Ebisu's other well-known contribution to the drinking pleasure of Japan. Foreigners are often curious about the name; it is derived from *cal*cium and sar*pis*, a Sanskrit word that connotes "most delicious taste." It came to Japan from Mongolia, the gift of an early entrepreneur who wished to supplement the limited Japanese diet with the beverage that the hard-riding Mongolian horsemen claimed was responsible for their "stamina," and after reading about snake medicine in the Shibuya chapter, you know how important that is to Japanese men. Mongolians might not recognize the resulting adaptation, a sweet, white base that is mixed with water (one part Calpis to four of water) and whose taste can be likened to sweetened yogurt. It is well thought of in Japan—in World War II, when everything was in short supply, the company was still in business manufacturing Calpis for the Imperial Navy. The company slogan, *Hatsukoi no Aji* (the taste of first love), has become a part of the popular language. The meaning: sweet and delicate.

Is Calpis good for you? Kaiun Mishima, founder of the company, died in 1974. Although officially retired, he still went to the office almost every day. He was ninety-seven.

Our next destination, Hiroo-cho, is known to many foreigners because of the Azabu Supermarket[2] and the International School of the Sacred Heart. And other places worth mentioning.

There is, for example, Shoun-ji (祥雲寺), a temple tucked away

---

1. Sapporo Brewery Co., 1–4–1 Mita, Meguro-ku; tel. 441–3181
   サッポロビール株式会社恵比寿工場　目黒区三田 1-4-1
2. Azabu Supermarket, 4–5–2 Minami Azabu, Minato-ku; tel. 442–3181
   麻布スーパーマーケット　港区南麻布 4-5-2

1. Sapporo Brewery
2. American Bridge
3. Sacred Heart (Int'l.) School
4. Azabu Supermarket
5. Shoun-ji

6. Hanezawa Garden
7. Kyodo Bunkakan
8. Tokiwa pine
9. Hikawa Jinja
10. Onko Gakkai

in a corner of a neighborhood shopping street. Enter through the Sammon (Mountain Gate) to discover an expansive cemetery completely covering a secluded hillside. A number of well-known daimyo are buried here, as well as medical doctors famous during the Tokugawa period. At that time Western medicine was practiced with the help of rare Dutch books, the only source of knowledge available during a period when contact with foreign countries was almost completely prohibited.

Japan has long lived in fear of earthquakes and fires. In 1900–01 the people also had to contend with the horror of bubonic plague. Perhaps the rats that carried it arrived on the foreign ships that were by then crowding the Port of Tokyo, now opened to the West. The city fought the spread of the disease by paying a bounty for each dead rat turned in. Yet, by 1903, it was felt that some memorial should be erected in memory of these dead creatures, and a spot was set aside within the Shoun-ji grounds for a monument to the rats whose lives were sacrificed for the safety of the city.

Rats, incidentally, are not viewed in Japan with the repugnance usually associated with them in the West. In the old days it was only a rich man who could afford rats; others were so careful of the scanty amount of food available that no rat would wait around for its share. There wouldn't be even one grain of rice left uncounted. Consequently, if you had rats, you had to be rich. That's why you often see them pictured on kakemono (hanging scroll paintings) at New Year's time. They are symbolic of the New Year's wish for wealth and, presumably, happiness.

Our tour would be simpler if temple cemeteries had back exits. Few of them do, so you must go around the outside of Shoun-ji to find Hanezawa Garden,[3] once the estate of Korekimi Nakamura, president of the South Manchuria Railway Company. The gate at the entrance is made of hinoki (Japanese cypress), now so expensive that few could afford so pretentious an entranceway. The Japanese-style house and garden are popular for wedding receptions and Japanese dinners. In the summer months, a corner of the attractive garden becomes a beer garden, a cool and quiet place to pause before proceeding to . . .

The Kyodo Bunkakan,[4] a local museum showing how people lived on the Yoyogi Plains (that's where you are) thousands of years

3. Hanezawa Garden, 3–12–15 Hiroo, Shibuya-ku; tel. 400–2013
   羽沢ガーデン　渋谷区広尾 3-12-15
4. Kyodo Bunkakan, 4–9–1 Higashi, Shibuya-ku; tel. 407–8615
   郷土文化館　渋谷区東 4-9-1

ago. From more modern times, there's a section of the wooden waterway that once brought water to Edo from the Tamagawa River and a treasured guide to the area showing houseowners, their names, seals, and even how much each paid in taxes. This valuable record, along with a number of the old books on display, was discovered in the house of a neighborhood sakè dealer. There's a poster too that shows protest movements aren't new to Japan. That man depicted with his fist raised in defiance is objecting to the dust that blew in from what is now Yoyogi Park and was then a parade ground for the military. Houseowners wanted the army to take its horses, heavy equipment, and drilling troops elsewhere.

Across the street is a marker locating the Tokiwa matsu (pine). Tokiwa was a lovely lady of the days that are recorded in *The Heike Story*, a novel based on the colorful events that occurred some eight hundred years ago. She once visited the lord of Shibuya Castle located nearby and sentimentally planted a pine tree to commemorate the occasion. Since then, there has always been a pine at the spot. Today's tree is in front of Pinedale, an apartment constructed by Homat Homes, a company that has contributed greatly to building an architectural bridge between East and West.

There's no hint of a castle anymore, yet there's something similar. Behind Pinedale is the walled estate of Prince Hitachi, the emperor's second son. It could be called a modern castle.

On down the street is Hikawa Jinja (永川神社), famous in early days for the open-air sumo matches that were held here every September. It's easy to locate the spot, a hollow in the hills where viewers must have spread out their mats and settled down with sakè and obento (boxed lunch) to enjoy the performance.

Finally, another museum, a tribute to a gentleman whose statue you'll see in front of the Onko Gakkai (温故学会), Hall of Memories. Hokiichi Hanawa was a blind scholar with a phenomenal memory. He devoted more than forty years of his life to reciting books which had been read to him years before. The books themselves were no longer available and his dictations allowed their preservation. You can see the results of his labor today in a library holding 17,244 woodblocks for printing. If you like, you can have a print made from one of them for a few hundred yen.

WINTER AUSTERITIES

Meguro: Black Eyes

AND HERE'S ANOTHER AREA named for the god Fudo, this time a black-eyed one. First, only a short distance from the station, we'll take you to a very un-citylike destination, the National Park for Nature Study （国立自然教育園）, with streams, ponds, birds, trees, and shrubs, the closest one can come to a wilderness in Tokyo. It has a long history. Some 550 years ago, before the Tokugawa era, the land belonged to a wealthy local lord. Later it was successively owned by ruling or influential families until after the war, when it was opened to the public. It is hard to believe that such a natural refuge can be discovered so near the heart of the city. It is claimed that it maintains the feeling of the Musashino plains of days long gone.

Now retrace your steps and find another landmark of Meguro—Tokyo's, and perhaps the world's, most elaborate romance hotel, the Hotel Meguro Emperor.[1] You can't miss it with all those turrets, towers, and balconies in cream-colored stucco. Rooms are individually designed. One produces artificial rain, another has a $14,000 bed that rises in a mirror-lined cylinder. The wondrous capacities of electronics are exploited to new limits to activate furniture, lighting, and video equipment for the appreciative guests who value the discretion for which the hotel is also known.

Well, back to the temples. The name Gohyaku (500) Rakan-ji (五百羅漢寺) refers to the five hundred disciples of Buddha, the woodcarvings for which the temple is famous. Among them is a statue known as the Okoi Kannon, supposedly dating from the Kamakura period. It was named for Okoi, mistress of Taro Katsura, once the governor of Taiwan and a prime minister in the Meiji era. Like many mistresses of famous men, she followed the traditional retirement plan. After his death, she became a nun. The first woman to be admitted here, she started her own tradition. The temple is now exclusively for women. She is buried beneath her Kannon statue. Her grave is visited by many women and girls, but who knows whether they bring their romantic problems or their interest in women's lib?

Look for the huge fish-shaped thwacking board hanging beneath the temple roof which is beaten to announce the serving of meals. It is said facetiously that this is the only "serving" of fish available to the priests, whose temple diet is vegetarian. In the old days Shinagawa fishermen, when their luck was off, would borrow the fish and take it into the sea, believing this would improve their catch.

Shortly beyond is Ryusen-ji (滝泉寺), where the black-eyed Fudo

1. Hotel Meguro Emperor, 2–1–6 Shimo Meguro, Meguro-ku; tel. 494–1211
ホテル目黒エンペラー　目黒区下目黒 2-1-6

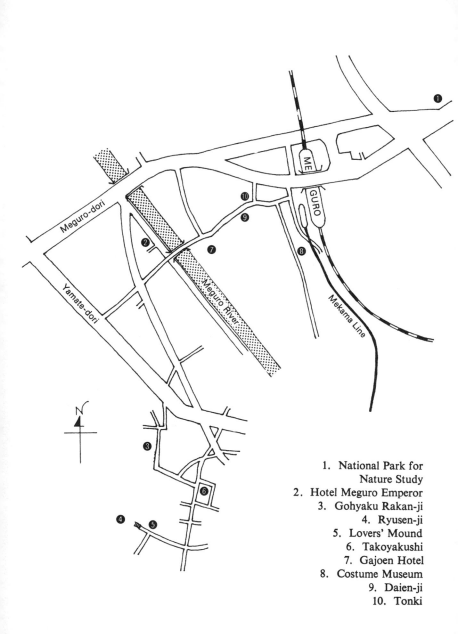

1. National Park for
   Nature Study
2. Hotel Meguro Emperor
3. Gohyaku Rakan-ji
4. Ryusen-ji
5. Lovers' Mound
6. Takoyakushi
7. Gajoen Hotel
8. Costume Museum
9. Daien-ji
10. Tonki

is enshrined. This deity's responsibility is to protect people from all misfortunes. Dreams figure in many of Japan's old stories. Jikaku Daishi, a famous 9th-century priest, dreamt about the god Fudo while resting here. Consequently it seemed appropriate to give Fudo-san a temple home at the place where the dream occurred.

It is also said that the priest held up a stick in the garden and a spring miraculously appeared. The water cascaded over rocks to form a waterfall. The waters are reported to have healing powers and through the years people have sat beneath them seeking cures for the illnesses of family members or friends—though many might become ill themselves from their efforts, since it is claimed that the colder the weather, the more likely the recovery. Even today during daikan, the coldest season, which begins in late January, people come to bathe in the freezing waters to demonstrate their strength of spirit.

The falls are still here, but one might wonder if the piped-in city water that presently flows over the stones holds the same magical powers as the earlier Fudo Falls.

On a hill behind the temple is a small gravestone that marks the resting place of Konyo Aoki, known in the Edo period for his Dutch studies. His real claim to fame, however, is for importing sweet potatoes from China and starting their cultivation in Japan, thus saving many people from starvation in those years when rice crops were lean but sweet potatoes grew strong. He is better known by the name of Kansho-sensei, Professor Sweet Potato.

To the left of the front gate of the temple you'll find a double "lovers' mound," the grave of Gompachi Shirai and Komurasaki, whose sad and romantic love story has been immortalized in song and drama. Such double graves are known as hiyokuzuka, named for the legendary one-winged, one-eyed bird which cannot fly until it finds its mate, an obvious symbol for lovers. But many who found their loves could not marry and chose double suicide as the only possible way of being together—in death. This was the predictable ending for the tragic romance of the fugitive samurai Gompachi and Komurasaki, a favorite courtesan of the Yoshiwara, the pleasure quarters of Edo.

Take the first left after paying your respects to the lovers for Takoyakushi (蛸薬師), temple of medicine. It was established in 840 by the priest Ennin. The diary of his China travels has been translated by former U.S. Ambassador to Japan, Dr. Edwin O. Reischauer. Title: *Ennin's Travels in T'ang China.*

Troubled by ibo? That's warts. If you rub them against the magic stone here, they will disappear. The stone came from China and it is supposed that it has/had some thaumaturgic mineral content. Some claim it is a meteorite.

There are several Jizo statues in the compound. They are the gift of Oshizu, the mistress of the second Tokugawa shogun. She prayed at this shrine that her son would be successful. He was. He founded the powerful Matsudaira family.

You might find a visit to the nearby Gajoen Hotel[2] interesting. Many will remember it as an Occupation hotel in the postwar period. The lobbies and halls are decorated with recessed paintings of yesterday's Japan, and the spectacular elevator doors show geisha scenes in mother-of-pearl, all splendid examples of Oriental rococo. Rates here are among Tokyo's most reasonable.

Quite in contrast is St. Anselm's Church,[3] a little further down and across the street, designed by Antonin Raymond who came to Japan with Frank Lloyd Wright and stayed.

Those interested in costumes through the ages will want to stop at the Costume Museum, a part of the Sugino School of Dressmaking.[4] Visitors are welcome, but it is necessary to phone in advance to have the building opened for you. Most of the clothing on display is European, from the fifteenth to eighteenth century.

---

2. Gajoen Kanko Hotel, 1–8–1 Shimo Meguro, Meguro-ku; tel. 491–0111
   雅叙園観光ホテル　目黒区下目黒 1-8-1
3. St. Anselm's Church, 4–6–22 Kamiosaki, Shinagawa-ku; tel. 491–5461
   聖アンセルモ教会　品川区上大崎 4-6-22
4. Sugino Costume Museum, 4–6–19 Kami Osaki, Shinagawa-ku; tel. 491–8151
   杉野学園衣装博物館　品川区上大崎 4-6-19

At our next temple stop, Daien-ji (大圓寺), you will find the grave of the priest Saiun, whose story is another of the bittersweet love tales of old Japan. According to one version, Saiun was one of the comely young boy companions of the priests at a temple in Komagome. The attractions of this life paled, however, when he met sweet Oshichi, whose family took refuge at the temple when their home was destroyed by one of the "flowers of Edo," the fires that frequently leveled large areas of the city. Oshichi longed for her lover when her family moved back to their rebuilt house. In an effort to reestablish those happier days, she set it afire. That was a serious crime in Edo, and she suffered the penalty applied automatically to all arsonists no matter how romantic their motivation. She was sentenced to death by fire. A saddened Saiun then joined the priesthood. "It's the least I can do for my beloved," history would have him say.

If it's time for lunch or supper and your choice is piping hot deep-fried pork, a tasty concoction known as tonkatsu, stop at Tonki.[5] No décor, just good food reasonably priced—and always crowds of people waiting to be served. There are three shops near the station. We have suggested the oldest and most famous. Many say it serves the best tonkatsu in all of Tokyo; others say in all of Japan.

Meguro was once famous for its many bamboos and a number of small restaurants were known for the local specialty, rice cooked with young bamboo shoots. An old man named Hikoshiro brought additional culinary fame to the area. He operated a small teashop on a hillside street slanting toward the Meguro River. The third shogun, Iemitsu, once stopped there for a rest while falcon hunting. He was served mackerel, the common fish whose greatest appeal has always been its reasonable price. Yet the mighty shogun, who could command the finest food of the realm, praised the old man

---

5. Tonki, 1-1-2 Shimo Meguro, Meguro-ku; tel. 491-9928
とんき　目黒区下目黒 1-1-2

elaborately, much to the amusement of his retainers, for what he claimed was the most delicious meal he had ever eaten. Perhaps he had never before been served mackerel, or any fish, cooked fresh from the sea. Food at the palace, on its long journey from kitchen to table, was passed by many tasters to eliminate any possibility of poisoning. Steaming hot fish just off the fire would have been a new experience.

五反田

ROOFTOP RECREATION

Gotanda: Five-Tan Rice Field

GOTANDA WAS another rice field, measuring five *tan*, or a little over an acre, in size. We've mentioned many other rice fields in this book but we haven't been able to show you even one. You won't find any here either; the paddies were all plowed under long ago. However, the willow-lined Meguro River that provided water for the paddies still flows through Gotanda. Today adjacent streets are filled with restaurants and sakè shops popular with the people who work in the area during the day and those who come home to Gotanda at night. Prices are relatively low and the wide variety will provide an

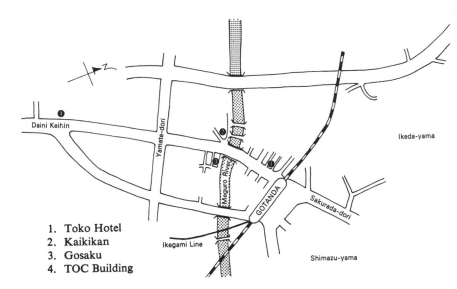

1. Toko Hotel
2. Kaikikan
3. Gosaku
4. TOC Building

introduction to just about everything you can eat and drink in Japan.

Notice the Toko Hotel[1] as you leave the station. It's one of the new businessmen's hotels with basic rooms, service, and prices. On down the street you'll see a more traditional kind of accommodation, the Kaikikan,[2] a ryokan (inn) that has stood here alongside the river for many years. The genkan (entranceway) unrolls a parasol-like ceiling which continues on down long corridors, demonstrating how many shades of beauty the Japanese can find in natural wood. At a ryokan, emphasis is placed on personal attention for the guest's comfort.

Also alongside the river, to the left, a well-known restaurant,

1. Toko Hotel, 2–6–8 Nishi Gotanda, Shinagawa-ku; tel. 494–1050
東興ホテル　品川区西五反田 2–6–8
2. Kaikikan, 2–22–6 Nishi Gotanda, Shinagawa-ku; tel. 491–1675
海喜館　品川区西五反田 2–22–6

Gosaku,[3] features dishes from Akita Prefecture. You'll find "mountain vegetables" in many of their specialties, nostalgic concoctions for Tokyo's country-at-heart city population. One of the most popular is shottsuru, "salty soup." It's much more tasty than it sounds, a not-so-salty fish or chicken stew cooked at your table. Ask, too, for kiri tampo, a rice cake toasted on a stick and added to the broth—along with lots of those mountain vegetables.

Our destination is the TOC Building,[4] Tokyo's merchandise mart. The initials stand for Tokyo Oroshiuri (wholesale) Center. It's a government project, supported by MITI, designed originally to relieve the congestion in the Nihon-bashi district. Opened in March, 1970, the building now provides office space for 380 companies and 7,700 people call it home during working hours.

Naturally, the center can provide the services of any small town. Maybe more. The basement holds a collection of restaurants of all kinds. There's a post office, a clinic, and a bank. You can park your car in the thousand-car garage or have it serviced at the gas station. And of course there are exhibition halls, conference rooms, warehouses, and a forwarding service. The top-floor French restaurant, Coq d'Or, can provide the French cuisine the name suggests as well as a cafeteria line at noon for a bargain meal of Japanese lunchtime favorites.

Each floor features a specialized type of merchandise although there is a lot of overlapping. The twelfth, for example, has ladies' ready-to-wear; the eleventh, men's clothes; the seventh, accessories; and the fifth, fabrics, women's lingerie, smoking goods, and gold and silver jewelry. Although these are the office-showrooms of wholesalers, many of them will sell directly and there are bargains to be had on all floors. Time your visit to the ladies' clothing section at sale time and you'll save an astonishing amount over the price

3. Gosaku Kaikan, 1–29–2 Nishi Gotanda, Shinagawa-ku; tel. 491–2221
   吾作会館　品川区西五反田 1-29-2
4. TOC (Tokyo Oroshiuri Center), 7–22–17 Nishi Gotanda, Shinagawa-ku;
   東京卸売センター　品川区西五反田 7-22-17　　　　　　　　tel. 494–2111

you'd pay at the regular retail outlets. You'll see the same things at Japan's finest department stores and specialty shops.

Explore as many floors as you can. Feel free to try your bargaining ability. You won't win them all, but you'll have enough success to make it worthwhile.

From the roof you can see Ikeda-yama, the mountain which once was the estate of the Ikeda daimyo family from Okayama, and Shimazu-yama, home of the Kyushu Shimazus. Both are still considered to be highly desirable residential areas. One of Japan's best-known women grew up in an Ikeda-yama mansion. The residence of the Shodas, parents of Michiko, wife of the crown prince, is located here. If you'd like to see it, devise some business with the Indonesian Embassy. It's across the street.

From your top-of-the-building vantage point, notice the several buildings that have made their roofs into gardens. At lunch time they will be filled with employees seeking fresh air and sunshine. TOC employees have a golf-driving range on the roof of their building. And a Shinto shrine.

Stop at the first-floor Gift Gate on your way back to the station. This is one of the main display rooms for Hallmark greeting cards. Think what fun you can have sending a familiar Hallmark card but with the message in Japanese. Let your friends wonder what you *really* mean.

大崎

SUBCONTRACTORS

Osaki: Big Cape

THIS WAS TO BE the station we skipped; Osaki has so little to offer a curious traveler. But then I spent a late-summer afternoon there and I'm not so sure. Perhaps you'll find something to interest you beyond that next bend in the road after all.

If you do get off the train, look to the left toward Shinagawa Station. You'll see a Sony factory in the midst of a metropolitan industrial complex. This is a showroom for the world-famous company's Trinitron color-TV sets. Sony's main office/factory with assembly lines for transistor radios and tape recorders is located in Shi-

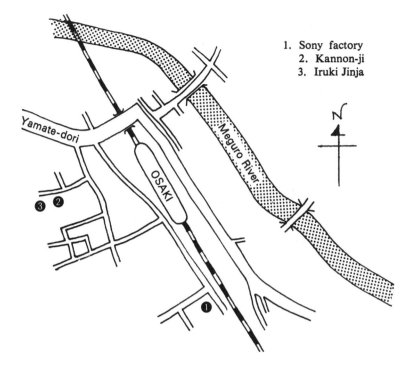

1. Sony factory
2. Kannon-ji
3. Iruki Jinja

baura, on the Tokyo Bay side of Shinagawa Station. Visitors are welcome, but advance notice is requested.[1]

From the overhead exit, you will see the glint of the blue-tile roof of a Buddhist temple in a small grove of trees. We have seen a lot of temples on this trip and there is nothing very special about this one except that it's rather unexpected to find it here among the factories. Whenever you are out exploring, head for the trees. If there is anything of interest, it will be there.

1. Sony Corp., 6–7–35 Kita Shinagawa, Shinagawa-ku; tel. 448–2175
   ソニー株式会社 品川区北品川 6–7–35

The roundabout route that leads to the temple will take you past a part of Tokyo that you have probably read about but perhaps never seen. Here are the small factories that depend on subcontracts from larger factories in the intricate web of Japanese industrial interrelationships. As you walk along the streets you can see the different segments of production, each an independent unit but each dependent upon the next-sized company above.

Stand at the foot of the well-worn steps leading up to the temple, Kannon-ji (観音寺). A wooden gate in need of repair hides the bright blue roof you saw from the station. You can climb the steps, past the cemetery with its moss-covered stone monuments and wooden name tablets (sotoba) silvered by sun and rain, forgetting for the moment that you are surrounded by factories. The concrete buildings at the top of the hill are new, a delayed postwar construction project to replace the old ones that were burned in an air raid.

Naturally, there is a shrine behind the temple. Iruki Jinja (居木神社) was a wartime casualty, and for many years there was only a worn and weathered substitute for the original. Now a new building has been completed. For years, there was a picture of the new shrine in the courtyard. Now it is a reality.

Here in the hills—from the station you couldn't sense the height of these rises beyond the tracks—are little houses, the streets, paved with stones, hardly more than paths. Even so, you must be wary of the ubiquitous small delivery trucks. We haven't got *that* far from the factories.

Walking on up the hill, seeking the trees off to the left, you may find yourself in front of an impressive gate. If it's open, you can look inside for a glimpse of a well-kept, Japanese-style estate, a holdover from another day.

Such contrasts are everywhere. Osaki—the name means "big cape"—was probably an apt description of this bayside area not so many years ago. Industrialization has a short history in Japan. Once these hilltops provided views of rice fields and thatch-roofed houses.

Later wealthy merchants and industrialists built their houses here. Now only a few remain, hidden away behind walls that shield them from the adjacent factory or apartment house.

I found one more as I headed back toward the station. At the top of a steep, tree-lined drive, there was another wall, another entranceway. I peeked through a crack and saw a deserted mansion. The small door at the side was unlocked, so I pushed it open and went inside. An ornamental wooden gate with a roof of cedar bark still stood as guardian to a garden, though the bamboo fence that once completed the barrier had long since fallen. There, among weeds taller than I, a dry riverbed was outlined with huge stones, each a treasure of great worth in a country that places the value of garden rocks in the millions of yen. There were towering stone lanterns too, and even in its overgrown state, the garden shared its beauty. Or perhaps the feeling was there *because* it was deserted, uncared for.

You may have heard the word *sabishii*. It means to be lonely; it suggests the desolate, the forlorn. It has an even deeper feeling, though, than these words imply. It also suggests a poignant sorrow. The word was an appropriate one for this house, I thought, as I sat in the quiet garden listening to the cicadas, the semi, singing their song of fall. Fall is always a sabishii season, an ending. But I had seen something else that made the old, empty house sabishii. There on the porch was a plant, its blossoms withered, its leaves brown and dried. Some delivery boy had left it there, following the instructions on the now-faded card. Because it was a morning-glory plant, I could guess about when it was delivered. Morning glories are appropriate gifts for early summer. But then, perhaps the delivery wasn't a mistake. Some past memory may have prompted the gift of this special flower to an empty house. Or perhaps somewhere else someone waited for a gift that never came.

It was all very sabishii, loneliness tinged with sorrow. I could also sense the outer edges of sadness, a rekindling of joy, for everywhere there must be a balance.

It was enough. I had no wish to explore other paths. The house I saw is likely demolished by now; property does not remain unused long in Japan. But there are many other places where you can know sabishii. Be receptive to them as you travel along the back streets of our city.

呂川

DECEMBER VENGEANCE

Shinagawa: Merchandise River

YOUR IMAGINATION will have to create lost images if you are to visualize the days when Shinagawa was the first stop along the old Tokaido highway that linked Edo to Kyoto. The long journey began at Nihon-bashi, and many travelers were ready to stop for the night by the time they reached Shinagawa. If you traveled by kago, a boxlike contraption carried on the shoulders of hearty retainers (you would be sitting, of course, on a tatami-matted floor), you might also be longing for a rest before beginning the more arduous part of your journey. Likely, too, there would have been tea and sakè breaks along the way.

174

Old Shinagawa was filled with inns, teahouses, and sakè shops, most of which were equipped to cater to the varied desires of men in search of amusements—Japan's reputation as a man's world has a long history. Guests in this "floating world of pleasure" were not only the travelers. There were also priests from nearby temples and samurai who made their home in Tokyo while their masters were doing their alternate service in the capital, the every-other-year-away-from-home that was so effective in preventing uprisings that might be contrived by daimyo left undisturbed in distant provinces. Shinagawa was especially popular with the men from Kagoshima, known for their quick tempers and independence. The system of rotating households could never completely eliminate their inclination to upset the early-day establishment, even if the confrontation was nothing more than a street brawl after an evening of drinking.

Shinagawa Station, recently renovated, needed it. The original building was constructed in 1872, Tokyo's first train station. You can have an aerial tour of the area from the Sky Lounge on the thirtieth floor of the Pacific Hotel (just across the street), which provides a spectacular panorama of what has happened since Shinagawa Station was a favorite destination for visitors from all over the country who came to view in awe the steam engines that puffed along from Yokohama all the way to Shinagawa and, in time, Akabane.

There were other attractions. The nearby seashore with clean beaches and clear waters lured visitors who enjoyed their boxed lunches beneath the pine trees that lined the shores. There were many besso—vacation villas—on the Shinagawa hill, which provided spectacular views of the bay.

What remains? The name by which the area is still known, Go-ten-yama, which means a mountain with besso. A few old houses hidden behind crumbling walls on the hillside. And, amidst the hotels, bowling alleys, office buildings, and shops, you'll find occasional mementos of the past, or worthy additions of more recent

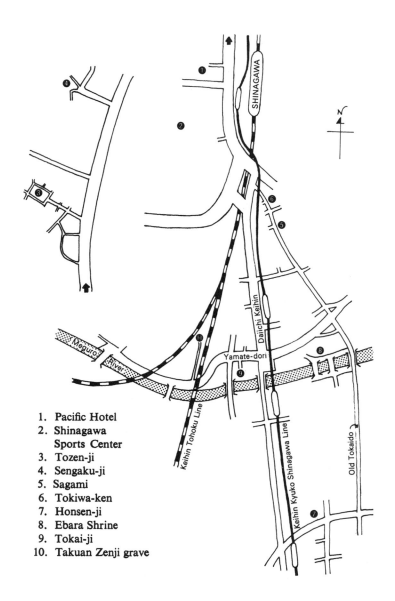

1. Pacific Hotel
2. Shinagawa
   Sports Center
3. Tozen-ji
4. Sengaku-ji
5. Sagami
6. Tokiwa-ken
7. Honsen-ji
8. Ebara Shrine
9. Tokai-ji
10. Takuan Zenji grave

times. Among the latter is the Shinagawa Sports Center,[1] with an impressive variety of activities for sportspeople and families, and the impressive marble-palace-like new hotel, hall, all part of the Seibu empire of department stores, leisure centers, and Prince Hotels, which are all located on princely old estates.

Back to earlier days. You think the housing situation is critical now. The first foreigners to come to Japan had their own problems, mainly that there was nothing that even faintly resembled a Western-style residence. Frequently temples were pressed into use to accommodate officials from abroad. The Zen temple Tozen-ji (東禅寺) was the address of the British consulate established in Tokyo in 1859. It was not an altogether satisfactory arrangement. The first British minister, Sir Rutherford Alcock, escaped death by hiding in the bath when retainers from the Mito clan (one of the three families from which the shogun could be selected) attacked the temple seeking vengeance. It seems that Alcock, a foreigner, had defied the sacredness of Mount Fuji by climbing to the holy summit. Later, under his successor, the Japanese guards who were assigned to protect the consulate attacked their British counterparts. Feeling that a temple was not necessarily a haven, the British moved soon after to their own building at Ikeda-yama near Gotanda. A stone by the gate of Tozen-ji notes its early association with the British.

Sengaku-ji (泉岳寺) is a pilgrimage point for many Japanese, especially at the year end. Here, on a snowy December night in 1702, was enacted one of the country's greatest dramas, that of the forty-seven ronin (masterless samurai) who avenged their former master. Naganori Asano, a daimyo from Ako, had died by seppuku (ritual suicide, perhaps better known in the west as harakiri) because of improper behavior at the shogun's court. The calm and gentle man had finally, in frustration and anger, drawn his sword

1. Shinagawa Sports Center 4–10–30 Takanawa, Minato-ku; tel. 440–1111 (Shinagawa Prince Hotel)
品川スポーツセンター　港区高輪 4-10-30

within the shogun's palace to threaten the life of Yoshinaka Kira, the smug protocol master who had advised him poorly on matters of behavior, thus leading to his disgrace. Because he had defied the regulation against displaying weapons in the palace, death by his own hand was obligatory.

Revenge was a long and carefully planned campaign by Asano's most loyal retainers. They paid the price for their success—the beheading of Kira—by themselves committing seppuku. The youngest ronin was seventeen, the oldest, seventy-seven. The retainers are properly reunited with their lord in death; their graves at the temple are arranged near his in order of precedence.

Many of the relics of the forty-seven ronin can be seen in one of the temple buildings, and a small shop, Koizumi Gishido, in front of the temple sells souvenirs, among them a miniature copy of the drum that summoned them to their rendezvous with vengeance that winter night.

For more of this story that demonstrates the Japanese concept of loyalty, see the Kabuki play *Chushingura*, which is always presented in December, or read any of the many historical accounts that have been published.

Remembering those days, let's go back and walk along what's left of the path the conspirators often traveled as they planned their revenge, now a narrow and irregular street which, for a kilometer or so, follows the course of the old Tokaido. Still crowded, yes, but with a far different citizenry than in earlier days when teahouses and brothels lined the streets. You will have to look hard for reminders of those days. There are a few old houses and some of Tokyo's least expensive inns. The most famous, the Sagami, once known for intrigues and romances, can now only be seen on TV. It recently disappeared into a new construction project.

The nearness of Shinagawa Station led to the development of a home industry that brought a different kind of fame to this area. It became a center for obento making. One of the original shops, Tokiwa-ken,[2] is still located here. If you look interested and hungry, they might even sell you one of their boxed lunches though most business is now on a contract basis.

Austrians may want to pause a while at Honsen-ji (品川寺) to see the temple's distinguished bell. It was sent to Vienna for the World Exhibition in 1873. And there it stayed for fifty-five years before it was finally sent back home. In those days, when few Japanese ever went abroad, it was regarded as a well-traveled, international bell.

After visiting the new/old Tokaido, you may long for the days of scenic seashores and fishing boats. Share your nostalgia with Ebara Shrine (荏原神社). Someone a long time ago (please don't ask for details) picked up a wooden mask on the beach. That night he dreamed that if he carried the mask into the water, local fishermen would suffer no disasters at sea and their catches would be bountiful. To commemorate that fortuitous revelation, the shrine notes the date with a Kappa Matsuri each June. Except for a few years when polluted seas made the event unfeasible, local fishermen and shopkeepers carry the omikoshi (portable shrine) to sea in a procession of boats filled with happy celebrants. Spurred on by tradition and sakè, they give the shrine its annual dunking. If you make arrangements in advance, you can be assured of a seat in one of the boats. Nearby Shinagawa Shrine celebrates on the same day, and the streets are filled with people, portable shrines, and festival carts. Be there if you can.

Ebara has another niche in history. When Emperor Meiji first came to Tokyo from Kyoto, he chose this shrine as a resting place where his retainers could prepare for his historic and colorful entrance into the city.

Those who fancy Japanese pickles will make a pilgrimage to

2. Tokiwa-ken, 1–3–25 Kita Shinagawa, Shinagawa-ku; tel. 471–4700
   常盤軒 品川区北品川 1-3-25

Tokai-ji (東海寺) to pay their respects at the grave of a celebrated priest, Takuan Zenji. An honored religious teacher, Takuan was a friend to the first three Tokugawas and gave his name to pickled radishes, which he developed as a food conveniently carried by samurai on long journeys. It is necessary to put a heavy weight on the radishes during pickling, and a stone is often used for this purpose. Takuan's grave is not hard to spot. It is topped with a pickling stone.

Nearby is a memorial tablet dedicated to the Japanese National Railways, and the tomb of Viscount Masaru Inoue, the Japanese official who was responsible for the establishment of Japan's first national railways. It was felt appropriate that he be near the place where it all started, and on a hill where he could watch with pride the sleek trains of the New Tokaido Line, the world's first high-speed railway, streak by.

田町

CHECKPOINT

Tamachi: Rice-Field Town

AGAIN THE STATION'S NAME suggests rice fields, but the early popularity of this area should have inspired something more picturesque for a name. The station stands where waves once met the sandy beaches, where people on fishing excursions came to cook their catches beneath the pines that lined the shore.

For visitors, today's Tamachi is little more than a brief stop along the Yamanote Line. Foreign residents may find the area looks familiar. It's not far from the old Immigration Office, where visa problems are hopefully resolved. The new office is in Ikebukuro.

Northeast of the station is an impressive building, the sports

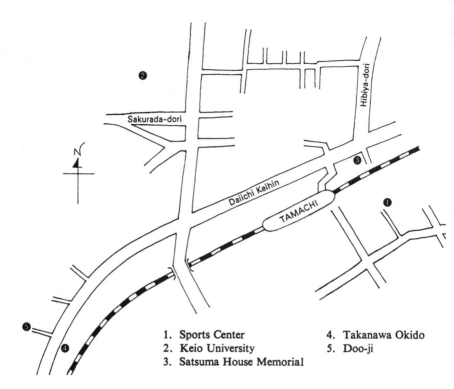

1. Sports Center
2. Keio University
3. Satsuma House Memorial
4. Takanawa Okido
5. Doo-ji

center for Minato Ward, a manifestation of the current interest in social welfare. With a swimming pool, roller-skating rink, gymnasium, and rooms for practicing and mastering various sports-related activities, the center provides facilities that until recently were usually found in shabby buildings and asphalt-covered playgrounds.

In the other direction from the station is Keio, one of Japan's oldest universities, founded in 1858. There are programs for foreign students, but first they must be able to understand lectures in Japanese. If they can't, they can enroll in the Japanese-language course.

But each station must have an itinerary. We have one. We'll ask you to turn right at the wide street, Daiichi Keihin, and walk along until you reach the eight-story Mitsubishi Building at the Hibiya-dori intersection. You'll find a plaque that marks the location of Satsuma House (薩摩屋敷), gathering place for the Satsuma clan and the setting for the meeting between Kaishu Katsu and Takamori Saigo when they discussed the peaceful turning over of Edo Castle at the time of the Meiji Restoration. You'll see this meeting pictured on the plaque. There's a map too, but it doesn't show today's city. It depicts instead the residences of the various neighborhood daimyo, familiar names such as Oda, Naito, and Matsudaira, and marks the location of old temples and shrines.

Don't look for them today. Instead, you can see a bit of carefully protected wall. Retrace your steps, pass the station, and head toward Shinagawa. Before long, on the left, you'll find a mound of grass-covered stones. This is the site of Takanawa Okido (高輪大木戸), a gate in the wall showing the boundary of Edo, a checkpoint on the route out of the city. Only those with permission to travel could go beyond this point. It was the custom for family and friends to travel as far as the gate. Many sad scenes of farewell were enacted here, for the roads were dangerous and trips were long. Perhaps these excursions to the city gate laid the foundation for the arrival and departure scenes we see today at Tokyo's airport with large groups of friends and relatives gathering together in the lobby and often holding aloft a brightly decorated banner emblazoned with the traveler's name.

If you'd care to linger a bit longer in the past, cross the highway and walk along the narrow street to Doo-ji (道住寺), a temple whose history dates back to the days when the wall was guardian for the city. Many must have stopped here to pray for the safe return of their loved ones.

浜松町

SEASIDE GARDEN

Hamamatsucho: Pine-Beach Town

STOP A MOMENT to look at the maze of tracks that is Hamamatsucho Station. You'll find it hard to believe that one of Tokyo's oldest gardens is alongside. The city was quite different in 1624 when what is now Shiba Palace Garden (Shiba Rikyu Onshi Teien, 芝離宮恩賜庭園) was presented to Yoshiaki Kato, the daimyo from Kii Province, for his Edo homestead. Later it was transferred to Tadamoto Okubo, who brought gardeners from his home province of Odawara to create a garden with miniature landscapes of famous mountains and a pond, connected to the sea, that rises and falls with the flow of the tides. It served the Tokugawa shoguns as a seaside re-

184

treat and later, after the Meiji Restoration, was designated as a "detached palace" of the Imperial Household. In 1924 it was given to the city of Tokyo to commemorate the marriage of Emperor Hirohito. Now tall buildings and cement embankments cover what once were empty, wind-swept beaches, and slightly muffled traffic noises have replaced the lonesome call of the gulls. As you walk along the paths that encircle the pond with its artificial islands and admire the spectacular stone lanterns, you will be grateful for this little pocket of resistance to urban sprawl, and you will perhaps want to offer a few words of thanks to the gardeners of Odawara who left their much-appreciated mark behind.

Next stop, Takeshiba Pier, a taking-off point for short harbor trips or cruises to more distant destinations such as Izu, Oshima, and Hachijo-jima. In the summer there are evening excursions with imaginative names, such as Joy-Joy Trip.[1]

For shorter trips, catch a water taxi to Asakusa, to Harumi International Fair Grounds, or to the Maritime Museum,[2] the huge white boatlike building you can see off to the right, an exciting excursion for you and/or the children.

There are plans to turn the waterfront into a parkway. The recently opened JNR Shiba Yayoi Hotel, with the latest facilities for conventions and spectacular views from the topfloor dining room, is part of the beautification project.

As you watch the huge freighters from many countries, the planes circling Haneda, and the waters stretching into the distance, you may forget, at least for a moment, that the center of Tokyo is only a few stations away.

Now you must retrace your steps, passing the station and heading for the huge red gate of Zojo-ji temple (増上寺). A right turn before the red torii outer gate—Daimon (大門)—will take you to

1. Tokai Kisen, 1–9–15 Kaigan, Minato-ku; tel. 432–4551
   東海汽船株式会社　港区海岸 1–9–15
2. Museum of Maritime Science, 13–1 Ariake-chi-saki, Koto-ku; tel. 528–1111
   船の科学館　江東区有明地先 13–1

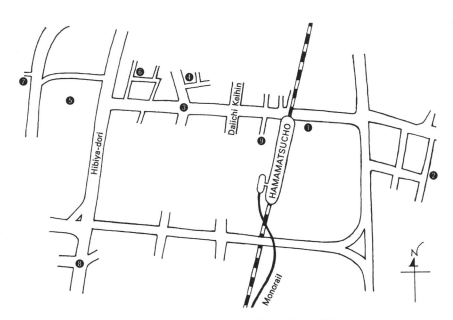

1. Shiba Palace Garden
2. Takeshiba Pier
3. Daimon
4. Shimmei Shrine
5. Zojo-ji
6. Minato Ward Office
7. Tokyo Tower
8. Shibazono-bashi exit
9. Tokyo World Trade Center

Shimmei Shrine (神明神社). See it up there, perched on top of a parking building, a sad reminder of changing times. This was once one of the most popular resting places for visitors who came to admire the splendors of Zojo-ji. They could only look, however, for Zojo-ji was the temple favored by the Tokugawa shoguns, and common people could not pass beyond its guarding gate.

There was, however, a hearty welcome for everyone at Shimmei. You may have noticed in the telling of this Tokyo tale how entertainment and pleasure districts sprang up around temples and shrines. This area was once filled with teahouses and other establishments and shops catering to travelers. Today the shrine precincts have shrunk and it relies on modern innovations for support, but its crossbeams still point hopefully toward heaven. You'll find a few secluded teahouse-type restaurants on the back streets, popular as meeting places for those who must be discreet. Many Kabuki scenes are laid in the lanes that led to Shimmei Shrine.

Now return to Daimon (Great Gate), not so great any more when you see the traffic congestion its narrow opening creates. It was indeed great when the passing throngs came by foot or palanquin. It's good to know that efforts to remove it have been stopped by people who prefer tradition to convenience. Once a ryokan stood alongside the gate, providing a haven for temple visitors, but requirements change. It has been replaced by a businessman's hotel, and traditional service has given way to automatic dispensers and meal tickets.

It is said that the first shogun, Ieyasu, chanced to meet the abbot Seiyo during his first day in Edo and spent the night at his temple. Greatly impressed by the abbot's knowledge, Ieyasu asked him to change to the Jodo sect and to preside at Zojo-ji, the head temple, which was then moved to Shiba, its present location.

Shiba means "grass," but you'll find little of it in the recently reconstructed Zojo-ji precincts. The old two-story Sammon gate has been restored along the original plan and is designated as an Important Cultural Property. It was built in 1605 in accordance with Ieyasu's wishes. Its name Sammon stands both for the three (san) sections of the gate and the three ways to salvation: wisdom, benevolence, and Buddha. Many foreign residents know the corner well. Across the street is the Minato Ward Office, where those who live in some of Tokyo's most popular residential areas must go for their alien-registration cards.

The temple is a copy of the original but is built of the most modern materials, as befits its latest reconstruction date, 1975. It boasts an underground parking lot, a revenue-raising convenience for visitors. At garage level is a complex of compact vaults, an answer to the problem of housing the dead in a crowded city. The enterprise, managed by a large department-store chain, has not proved especially popular. "We must live in apartments all our lives," people say, "and we don't want to be stacked up after we die too."

Usually on display at the temple is the genealogical chart of the Tokugawa shoguns. The long lines show the number of children and wives. Look for the longest and you'll find the record of the eleventh shogun. He produced fifty-five children, seven of them by Ocho, obviously one of his favorite mistresses.

The huge temple bell, more than three meters high, was completed in 1673. It weighs fifteen tons and is known as the one-league bell, though no one today seems to know whether it's because it could be heard a league away (some said you could hear it clear across the bay in Chiba) or because a man could walk a full league while the sound was dying away.

Not so long ago this was a quiet, rather overgrown area of moss-covered stone lanterns and old buildings. Only a trace of this remains; it can be glimpsed behind the main temple building. Other monuments have been moved away, and today, on what was once temple grounds, you'll find a golf-driving range, hotels, and that great metropolitan marker, Tokyo Tower. If you want the tower view, go up at twilight and stay for the great Tokyo turn-on when the city becomes a sea of sparkling multi-colored lights. Much of this area is still known as Shiba Park, recognizable now and then by a clump of bushes or a path through a mini-woods. For a kaleidoscopic view of past and present, climb the hill behind the Shibazonobashi exit of the Shiba Koen Subway Station.

Something should be said about the Tokyo World Trade Center, the forty-story building adjacent to the station. The ideal of internationalism envisaged by the promoters has gotten lost somewhere along the way, but it's worth a visit for its concentrated example of the Japanese ability to take any concept and make it distinctly their own. Thus the collection of Japanese-style "foreign" restaurants in the basement, the international exhibits with all the signs in the local language, and the bargain-sale look of the shopping plaza. There's also an observation platform—buy a ticket to look—with its collection of souvenir stands, game machines, and refreshments, none of which can detract from the truly magnificent view—when you get to it. You'd probably prefer to stop at one of the top-floor restaurants where you can have the same view, but the best vantage point is reserved for members of the World Trade Center Club.

You can extend your Hamamatsucho visit by following the signs to the monorail that leads to Haneda Airport, quite a complete tour in itself. You'll see factories dumping their effluents into the canal, have an intimate view of the second-floor accommodations for race-track personnel conveniently located above the stables, and sigh to see the cars congestion-packed on the expressway. There are industrial complexes that you can overlook to see Tokyo Bay in the distance. And you can share all this with today's samurai, briefcases clutched between their legs, off to do battle in the boardrooms of Nagoya and Osaka and Kagoshima. Or perhaps your companions are vacationers heading for the clear waters and sandy shores on distant Japanese islands, or people returning to their "umareta tokoro"—the place where they were born—for family reunions.

Until 1975, Haneda Airport served both domestic and international travelers. Now China Airlines is the only foreign line permitted to use Haneda, the fortuitous result of an agreement with Mainland China that the two should not share facilities. This has proved to be a distinct advantage for the Taiwan line, whose passengers are spared the long trip to Narita. You can read the story of the new international airport in the chapter, "The Other Side of Narita" in our second volume, *More Foot-loose in Tokyo*.

LOCKSMITH ART

Shimbashi: New Bridge

SHIMBASHI MIRRORS the face of Tokyo's common man. Narrow streets near the station make up for their short length by the vertical expanse of the innumerable signs advertising a conglomerate of bars, restaurants, and nightclubs. Pachinko parlors lure the every-man gambler, and coffee shops provide Japanese-style privacy for intimate meetings. "International shopping" with the inevitable ninety-nine percent locally oriented merchandise is featured at the Shimbashi Center under the expressway across Sotobori-dori and in the office-building arcades. The emphasis is on bargains, often at the expense of quality.

Near the station is Takumi,[1] a shop that shows quite a different aspect of merchandising. Here you will find a broad selection of Japanese folkcrafts, common goods of pottery, paper, fabric, and wood, all demonstrating the Japanese appreciation for simple, functional products. Takumi, now more than forty years old, was Japan's first folkcraft store. It also serves as headquarters for the Japan Folkcraft Society and is closely affiliated with the Japan Folkcrafts Museum, described in the Shibuya chapter.

Hori,[2] the first shop to provide Western locksmithing, also chose Shimbashi as its location and still provides services and products that are not generally available, such as fireplace screens (most fireplaces in Japan are fitted for gas heaters and don't need them). Ask to see the fascinating collection of locks from all over the world in the second-floor museum. None can match Japanese locks for beauty. Designed for tansu (chests), they are shaped like dragonflies, fish, or eggplants. There's a showcase on the first floor with examples of specialty locks. One is a chastity belt.

In 1882 the road from Shimbashi through the Ginza was paved with bricks to accommodate the new horse-drawn streetcars. The charge was three sen for first-class passengers, two sen for others. Neither trunks nor baggage would be accommodated, but children could ride free of charge. Those wanting to board stepped into the street and raised their hands, just as we do today for taxis.

The name Shimbashi means "new bridge," but that was many years ago. The bridge is long gone. Even the water it spanned has now been relegated to an underground passage beneath the highways.

Evening is best for exploring the colorful side streets, where you can enjoy a variety of food and drink and companionship for prices considered modest in Tokyo—but be careful. There are also the

1. Takumi Craft Shop, 8–4–2 Ginza, Chuo-ku; tel. 571–2017
   たくみ工芸店　中央区銀座 8–4–2
2. Hori Locks and Hardware Co., 2–5–2 Shimbashi, Minato-ku; tel. 591–6301
   堀商店　港区新橋 2–5–2

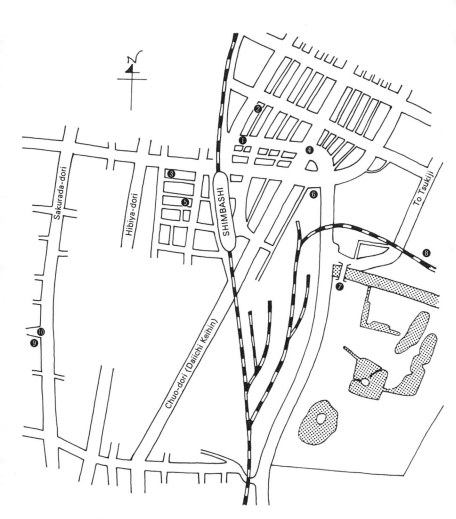

1. Shimbashi Center
2. Takumi
3. Hori
4. Shimbashi
5. Karasumori Shrine
6. Shiodome
7. Hama Detached Palace Garden
8. Tsukiji Wholesale Market
9. NHK Museum
10. Atago Shrine

familiar Japanese bars that make a practice of extortionate prices, and your expense allowance won't come close to covering them. Look for the places that seem to be frequented by Tokyo's unmistakable modest-salary man.

With luck and helpful directions you might find Karasumori Shrine.[3] It's down a bar-lined street so narrow you might not even see it if you are there—and you won't see much if you do. It's only a tiny compound encircled by cement. Once this was the neighborhood favorite, with crowds of people seeking the favor of the fox gods who have always been the protectors of those who live by their wits or their beauty.

Adjacent to the station is sprawling Shiodome (汐留), one of Japan's largest freight terminals. Near Shiodome's main entrance is a tiny park that commemorates a visit by Emperor Meiji when Japan's first train line was extended here from Yokohama and Shinagawa in 1872, having a total length of about twenty-five miles. And don't think everything was cheap in those good old days. Taking into account the purchasing power of money then and now (you can even figure it out in terms of rice if you want), a first-class ticket from Shimbashi to Yokohama cost about as much as today's Shinkansen fare from Tokyo to Osaka. Still preserved is a small section of the original track. There's a building nearby where you can take your packages for freight shipment throughout Japan. Some 3,750 tons of freight and cargo are handled daily at Shiodome.

Back on the main street, you may wonder at a building covered by small protrusions. Each is a prefabricated capsule apartment, a tiny but complete unit that anyone not bothered by claustrophobia could call home. Every tenant is entitled to one porthole-like window, a bed, a minute kitchen, and outlets for an assortment of electrical helpers.

3. Karasumori Jinja, 2–15–5 Shimbashi, Minato-ku; tel. 591–7865
烏森神社　港区新橋 2-15-5

Our destination is the Hama Detached Palace Garden (Hama Rikyu Onshi Teien, 浜離宮恩賜庭園). Its origin goes back more than three hundred years to the time when Tsunashige Matsudaira, Lord of Kofu Province, established a villa here. Its quiet beauty and expansive size defy Tokyo's reputation as a greenless city. Postcard-pretty bridges sheltered by wisteria trellises span the ponds that rise and fall along with the tides of Tokyo Bay. In earlier days, distinguished foreign guests were entertained here. Especially popular were the annual duck-netting parties.

Walk through the park, cross the bridges, and soon you will reach what once was the seashore. Now between buildings and embankments you can catch a tantalizing glimpse of the distant bay. There's a little hill from which, on a clear day, you can see—guess what!—Mount Fuji. Walk along the waterway to the back corner of the park where you can watch the boats go by on the Sumida River. And the amazing thing about it is that no matter what the weather or season, the park will be almost exclusively yours, so enjoy it at your leisure.

There's a back gate to the park reached easily from Hamamatsucho Station, but it's open only in "fine weather," and who's to judge that in Tokyo? We chose to include the Hama Garden on the Shimbashi tour so you can be sure of admittance.

On down the street from Shimbashi is Tsukiji (築地), the location of Tokyo's wholesale market for fish and vegetables (中央卸売市場). For excitement visit it early in the morning, around 5:30, while the fish auctions are under way. Stay out of the aisles when the sale is over, however. Those who are pulling fish carts to waiting trucks are not concerned about the welfare of tourists. You can't bid on the big fish—you won't even understand the chant that determines the going price—but you can shop at the stands inside the building where all the creatures of the sea are laid out in a still-life display that once again demonstrates the Japanese sensitivity to color, balance and design. Osushi lovers choose the shops near

Tsukiji fish market for their feasts when they want the freshest and the best.

Explore the streets adjacent to the fish market for the best of the day's products. Buy them for your own table.

Tsukiji—the word means "reclaimed land"—was once an area of mudflats at the mouth of the Sumida River. Later huge stones, much like those surrounding the palace moat, were used to build protecting walls. Shortly after the opening of Japan to the West, it was set aside as a special section for the foreigners who were arriving in increasing numbers. There were diplomats, missionaries, and traders, and one suspects that Tsukiji was chosen because it was set off from the city proper by the retaining walls and a number of canals, and thus a fitting (isolated) place for these strange people. Soon the area became an orderly, well-kept community with Western-style homes, churches, schools, hotels, and hospitals. Even then land was not cheap. A parcel with twenty-four small lots brought almost $30,000.

An early chronicler (Isabella Bird, in *Unbeaten Tracks in Japan*) remarked about the crowded conditions: "The roads are broad and neatly kept, but the aspect . . . is dull and desolate, and people live near enough to each other to be hourly fretted by the sight of each other's dreary doings. . . ."

The area had a rather short life as a foreign settlement—about thirty years. In 1899, foreigners were granted the right to hold land and to live outside the walls of Tsukiji.

You can return to the station by way of the Shimbashi Embujo,[4] or plan to go sometime when a Kabuki performance or a geisha dance recital is being held. The famous theater is situated in one of Tokyo's most illustrious geisha districts, the one favored by many of the government officials who plan the country's policies.

4. Shimbashi Embujo, 6–18–2 Ginza, Chuo-ku; tel. 541–2211
新橋演舞場　中央区銀座 6-18-2

Choose another direction from the station if you have a liking for the history of communications. Our destination is a bit distant, but still you should know of the NHK Museum[5] on top of Atago Hill. Here are many exhibits of the early days when Japan was establishing its communications network. In one room you can sit on a train seat and watch yourself watching the scenery go by on a nearby TV screen.

There are a number of access routes to the museum, including one for cars (you wind along an improbable tree-lined road) but perhaps the most historic—if your muscles are strong—is up the eighty-six steps to Atago Shrine. These are the male steps; there's a gentler female approach to the right with 107 steps.

Here's how the story goes. Back in 1634, the shogun Iemitsu saw an attractive spray of plum blossoms at the top of the hill. He ordered his mounted escorts to ride up the steps to pick them. Many tried, and the result was catastrophic for both horses and riders. Finally a samurai named Heikuro Magaki reached the top (though there is no record of how he got back down). We are told, however, that he was properly rewarded. Since then ten other riders have succeeded in scaling the stairs. One chose a special year for his assault—1925, the year the first radio station was opened on top of the hill. We don't know if the two events were related, but we can be sure that there were no plum blossoms. It was November.

---

5. NHK Museum, 1–10 Shiba Atago-cho, Minato-ku; tel. 433–5211
   NHK放送博物館　港区芝愛宕町 1–10

SOUNDS OF THE CITY

Yurakucho: Pleasure Town

YURAKUCHO PRESERVES the name of an all-but-forgotten daimyo, Oda Yurakusai, whose residence was once the only building of significance to be seen in this area, and it was of modest size. Today Yurakusai-san's holdings comprise the heart of the downtown shopping district, where emphasis always falls on whatever is new. Fashions just introduced in Paris or New York or Rome can be seen today along the Ginza. Shut your eyes and hear the sound of the city—not the cars or trains or ubiquitous loudspeakers, but the hurrying feet of the people who never seem to slow down, though

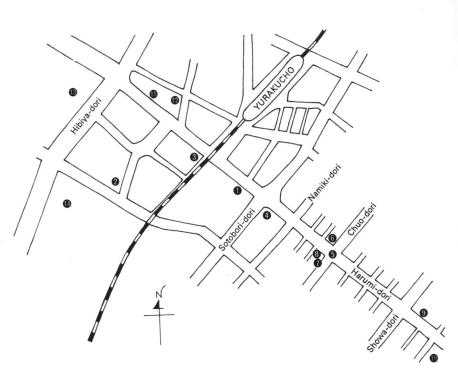

1. Sukiyabashi Park
2. Takarazuka Theater
3. Tourist Information Center
4. Sony Building
5. Ginza 4-chome
6. Wako
7. Kyukyodo
8. Jena
9. Kabuki Theater
10. Shimbashi Embujo
11. Hibiya Park Building
12. American Pharmacy
13. Hibiya Park
14. Imperial Hotel

occasionally they stop for a few moments to prepare for the next assault.

Once the station area under the tracks was crowded with a hundred or more tiny food and drink stands which gave it the name of Sushi Alley. In 1965 it was decided to "clean them out" (though you might wonder today if anyone ever did) as part of a modernization project. There is also a nearby park, Sukiyabashi. Watch a rock show, be asked to sign a peace petition by a dedicated student, or be presented with a gracious bow, or seasonal flowers, or vegetables from some distant prefecture. There are some who still remember the old days, and come back to Yurakucho to enjoy brief friendships over sakè and raw fish in what's left of Sushi Alley.

Leave from the West exit for the short walk to the Takarazuka, a theater of contrasts. On the fifth floor is the famous Nichigeki Music Hall with nude reviews that strive to be naughty but can only be nice because Japanese girls, even in burlesque, project an image of innocence. Downstairs are the sacchrine performances of the Takarazuka group with an all-girl cast enacting romantic spectaculars that appeal to Japanese school girls, whose admiration of the stars is a mix of worship and envy. James Michener's "Sayonara" has a Takarazuka girl as its heroine.

Back toward the station, on a corner near the overhead railway tracks is the Japan National Tourist Organization's Tourist Information Center,[2] where a knowledgeable staff can tell you what to do where in several languages. Slightly beyond is the Sony Building which usually features an attractive display on the corner. Four floors down is the exact replica of the Paris Maxim's, complete with red carpet and potted pines at the drive-up entrance in one of the city's largest underground parking lots with accommodations for more than eight hundred cars.

Continue eastward to what is probably Japan's most famous intersection, Ginza 4-chome, the heart of the internationally known Ginza. There are many department and specialty stores, among them Wako, perhaps the most prestigious and expensive. It is a part of K. Hattori and Company, known around the world for Seiko

1. Tokyo Takarazuka Theater, 1–1–3 Yuraku-cho, Chiyoda-ku; tel. 591–1211
東京宝塚劇場　千代田区有楽町 1-1-3
2. Tourist Information Center, Kotani Bldg., 1–6–6 Yuraku-cho, Chiyoda-ku;
国際観光振興会　千代田区有楽町 1-6-6 小谷ビル　　　　　　　tel. 502–1461

watches. There's a famous shop, Kyukyodo, near the corner, that sells only incense and exquisite papers, and another, Jena, that specializes in foreign books. You'll find a police box with polite attendants who will provide carefully drawn maps to wherever you want to go. The Ginza is also the entranceway to a nighttime world that can be either spectacular (nightclubs) or traditional (intimate bars and Japanese-style restaurants) along the willow-lined back streets.

The name Ginza dates back to the time when silver—*gin*—was minted here. It's been changing hands rapidly along Ginza streets ever since, as Tokyo citizens, reluctant to ask the cost of any item or service (because it might indicate concern over funds that they would prefer not to confess), crowd department stores and specialty shops or patronize the off-Ginza bars and nightclubs which can be disaster to the unknowledgeable. Your evening's entertainment may range from a couple thousand yen to several hundred thousand, and few foreigners will ever be able to judge which is which from appearances—or match the nonchalance of a Japanese who has just been handed a bill with one or even two more zeros than he expected.

The old days of Edo—woodblock prints come to life—are recreated on the stage of the Kabuki Theater.[3] The impressive building with its distinctive temple-like curved roof and bright decorations was rebuilt with contributions from people all over Japan during the early postwar years when few had anything to share. You can stay all day, enchanted by costumes and plot, dismayed at the slowness with which the story progresses. Visitors in a hurry can buy a ticket for a single act, though they'll view it from the rafters of the building. The tickets are appropriately named tachi-mi-seki (stand-and-see seat).

Go west from the station to pass the Hibiya Park Building, still known as the Nikkatsu Building to old-timers, an office building

3. Kabuki-za, 4–12–15 Ginza, Chuo-ku; tel. 541–3131
歌舞伎座　中央区銀座 4–12–15

with a recommendable downstairs shopping arcade and, on the back corner, the American Pharmacy,[4] which for years has supplied both Japanese and foreigners with hard-to-find imported pharmaceuticals, toiletries, and household goods.

When Tokyo was undertaking one of its earliest modernization programs, back in 1901, a giant ginkgo tree stood near the Hibiya crossing. It was sacrificed to a street-widening project. It was hard to find a buyer, but finally a firewood dealer bought it for ¥40. It proved to be no bargain. It took him 25 days to cut it up and haul it away at a cost of ¥450.

Hibiya Park was opened three years later, a part of the same city-beautification project. It's a popular place for the launching of local offensives, demonstrations protesting the rising cost of rice or the increase in electric rates. Columns of marchers set off up the hill for the prime minister's residence carrying placards and flags. In old Edo days too, protests were legal, but it was known that the leader must be willing to sacrifice his head for the privilege of filing the petition. Thus the people were guaranteed that their voice could be heard, but in a fashion that assured the continuance of the system by effectively discouraging complainers. (See the chapter on Narita in *More Foot-loose in Tokyo*.)

Across from the park is the Imperial Hotel, the new tower building 31 stories tall. It is difficult to say just how many "new" Imperials there have been. The first was opened in 1890. It was also one of the very first Western-style hotels in all of Japan and certainly the most splendid. The name was an easy choice, since the Imperial Household had been influential in seeing that the hotel was established so that the increasing number of foreign visitors could be appropriately accommodated. Of the many rebuildings and additions over the years, there can be no doubt that the best known was Frank Lloyd Wright's, recognized as one of the world's

4. American Pharmacy, Hibiya Park Bldg., 1–8–1 Yuraku-cho, Chiyoda-ku; アメリカンファーマシー　千代田区有楽町 1-8-1 日比谷パークビル　tel. 271-4034

great hotels until it was replaced by the previous "New Imperial" in 1970.

Wright's squat, ferroconcrete structure gained fame shortly after its completion when it withstood the devastating 1923 earthquake that all but leveled the city. It also established its fine reputation for service by helping to feed the thousands of homeless who settled in Hibiya Park for the duration of the emergency. It should be pointed out too that Wright's building had a tremendous influence on Japanese architecture, since the resilience of Western-style construction was so effectively demonstrated. You can see a few of the stones from Wright's Imperial preserved in the bar on the mezzanine. The entranceway of the old hotel, along with part of the lobby and the Garden Bar pond, has been rebuilt at Meiji-mura, a park near Nagoya that maintains outstanding examples of buildings from the Meiji era.

Before leaving the Imperial, we should mention that the older building has one of the best arcades in Tokyo, with outstanding shops such as Odawara (antiques) and Uyeda (jewelry). The arcade in the tower building displays name-brand imports.

We should also pay tribute to Tetsuzo Inumaru, Japan's most famous hotelier, at least until the Okura opened its doors. It was he who introduced the first "Viking service," a buffet table originally Scandinavian but which in Japan can be Swiss or Italian or even Chinese, for the name has spread throughout the country, and encompasses every cuisine. Mr. Inumaru chose the name, and to him the credit must go. He considered—but passed over—the name smorgasbord. Now try *that* in Japanese. Inumaru San did not live to see the newest Imperial. He died in 1980.

* * *

And now we have come to the end of our travels through Tokyo, if indeed it is ever possible to come to the end of a circle. We have visited many places, some famous, some little known, at the station stops along the Yamanote Line and through a thousand years of history.

Our iron-bound route has kept us from exploring other places in this vast, sprawling metropolis, but it would be impossible to include in one book all there is to see in the many small communities that make up the world's almost-largest city.

The around and around and around trips of the Yamanote Line could perhaps be chosen as an appropriate symbol of the Japanese people, always changing, always on the move, yet always returning to the place where they began, realizing that the destination is no more important than the place where they have been.

*   *   *

This was how we ended the first edition of *Foot-loose in Tokyo*. Our choice of the Yamanote Line for format kept us from exploring other destinations in this vast, sprawling metropolis, but it would be impossible to include in one book all that there is to see in the many small communities that make up our city.

Now, because some updating is necessary, in the original text, we have not only revised our original book, but have gone on to write a companion volume about our favorite places that are not along the Yamanote Line; it is entitled *More Foot-loose in Tokyo*, and it describes "Shitamachi," the old downtown area of Edo and Tokyo, where the past still lingers, and yesterdays are preserved while ways are found to accomodate the present. A chapter on Narita, the inconveniently located doorway to Tokyo, is included. It will provide the traveler with a multilayered introduction to Japan.

So, instead of closing the book and completing your tour, you can continue your exploration, criss-crossing the Yamanote Line by subway, to other destinations that will enrich your own Japanese experience.

Station-by-Station Finding List

This is the final page of Foot-loose in Tokyo, but there is no way that the story we tell can be ended. Japan is a country of rapid changes and what we see today will likely be gone tomorrow. It is comforting for the curious traveler that what is there instead will still be interesting -- and remain singularly Japanese.

Thus while our memories weave images of picturesque streets, brown wooden houses and miniscule gardens, our eyes report sweeping patterns created by overhead expressways and clusters of skyscrapers so automated that they are known as "intelligent buildings."

However can a guidebook to such a city be kept up-to-date?

Of course it can't, nor should it be. What's past is often of far more interest than the sterility of a modern city. So, if what you expected is not there, imagine how it once was and enjoy them both. There is also much to say for change. Shopkeepers may speak nostalgically of the past, but they would want that past recreated with TVs, air conditioners and central heating in a location three minutes from a subway.

And still, within the massive changes, reminders of the past remain. We shall choose pages 102-103 for our example. The first edition told you of the Ikebukuro Onsen, and we selected it for the chapter illustration. The revised edition noted that it had disappeared. Instead, we suggested a new-type bath, the Tokyo Bio Radon Center. Now, at the fourth printing, it, too, is gone, replaced by an office building.

Of course you could stay at the Dai-Ichi Ikebukuro Inn. That's where the Ikebukuro Onsen was. Even though each room has its own bath, today's guests continue, in a way, the old tradition. They, too, look to the communal bath for relaxation after a stressful day, only now it is a sauna.

As you explore today's Ikebukuro and all that's new, let your memory linger a bit with the old Ikebukuro Onsen.

You will find other changes as you follow your foot-loose path around our city, and note them well, for tommorow they will be something else, and you will be able to say, I remember when . . . .

ABOUT THE AUTHOR

JEAN PEARCE is a knowledgeable guide to cultural contrasts who has gained her insight during some 30 years of reporting and lecturing on Japan. She writes a widely read and often quoted twice-weekly column for the Japan Times, Japan's leading English-language newspaper, and contributes to other publications both in Japan and abroad. Her candid observations have earned her a reputation for exposing, with wit and wisdom, the opposites that exist between East and West. The emphasis is never on barriers, but rather on the different concepts that create them so that the barriers can become passageways to understanding.